THE JOURNEY OF CARLO MARTINI

I give special thanks to Chris Dalton for his determination and skills in helping me form my memories and words and photographs into a fine production that I am able to provide to my readers.

The Journey of Carlo Martini

Carlo Franco Martini

Grateful Steps
Asheville, North Carolina

Grateful Steps Foundation
30 Ben Lippen School Road #107
Asheville, North Carolina 28806

Copyright © 2015 by Carlo Martini

Library of Congress Control Number 2015904532

Martini, Carlo Franco
The Journey of Carlo Martini

All photographs are from the personal collection of the author
unless otherwise noted in the caption.

ISBN 978-1-935130-18-5 Paperback

Printed in the United States of America
at Lightning Source
FIRST EDITION

All rights reserved. No part of this book
may be reproduced in any manner whatsoever
without written permission from the author.

www.gratefulsteps.org

*Dedicated to the memories
of Mom and Dad*

CONTENTS

Author's Note   vi

Chapter 1   Apricale   1
Chapter 2   Bordighera   4
Chapter 3   First Voyage to America   9
Chapter 4   Back in Italy   11
Chapter 5   At the Movies as a Small Boy   15
Chapter 6   Meeting Elvis   18
Chapter 7   My First Autograph   23
Chapter 8   My Return to America   24
Chapter 9   Englishtown, New Jersey   26
Chapter 10   Jamesburg, New Jersey   30
Chapter 11   Talent Show at Middlesex County Fair   39
Chapter 12   Brotherhood of Magicians Ring 200   44
Chapter 13   The Move to Florida   49
Chapter 14   Nashville   51
Chapter 15   Sammy Davis Jr.   59
Chapter 16   Ohio   65
Chapter 17   Pittsburgh   69
Chapter 18   Backstage at the Grand Ole Opry   75
Chapter 19   A Gift for Elvis   80
Chapter 20   Graceland   86
Chapter 21   Elvis' Circle G Ranch   93
Chapter 22   Aunt Lorraine and Others in Elvis' Family   95

Contents

Chapter 23 Ginger Alden	98
Chapter 24 Jerry Lewis	101
Chapter 25 The Mike Douglas Show	105
Chapter 26 Frank Sinatra	108
Chapter 27 Future Stars on the Coast of Florida	112
Chapter 28 Ann-Margret	115
Chapter 29 Ann-Margret in Atlantic City	119
Chapter 30 Johnny Cash	121
Chapter 31 Australia	123
Chapter 32 The Home of Elvis' Father	128
Chapter 33 Ernest Tubb	131
Chapter 34 The Ernest Tubb Theatre	134
Chapter 35 Wrap around Nashville	137
Chapter 36 Back to Nashville	141
Chapter 37 Cher	148
Chapter 38 Paris	152
Chapter 39 The Day I Met Debra	155
Chapter 40 Western Movie Appearances	158
Chapter 41 Jones and Humperdinck	160
Chapter 42 On the Italian Riviera	165
Chapter 43 Sonny Schroyer	172
Chapter 44 Cherokee, North Carolina	177
Chapter 45 Back to Memphis	180
Acknowledgments	184

Apricale

My father, Settimo Martini, a farmer, was born in the village of Apricale in the hills not far from Sanremo, a city on the Italian Riviera. He was a cousin of Giovanni Martini, who was a bugler at the Battle of the Little Bighorn with General George Custer.

My mother was born in the city of Varapodio, Calabria, in the south of Italy. At the age of fifteen, my mother left Calabria to join her brother in Bordighera on the Riviera where he worked in a bread shop.

Original fountain
 Fountain in Varapodio where author's mother obtained buckets of water for household needs.

Fountain today.

When World War II broke out, her brother went to fight in the war, so she had to leave his apartment. Because she had no other place to go, she spent several months with nuns in a convent. After that, she worked in the villa of a colonel.

Apricale, photo by my sister Roseanne.

Giovanni Martini, who carried Colonel Custer's last message, had changed his name to John Martin. Photo used by permission from his family.

While working in the colonel's villa, she and a girlfriend, who later became my father's brother's wife, went one afternoon to the village of Apricale. That day her girlfriend introduced my mother to my father. One month later, in April 1944, they were married in an Apricale church.

World War II brought hard times. Everyone tried to survive. During the wedding of my parents, the Germans started coming into the village.

My parents were taken by surprise and didn't know what to do, so they escaped and went to live in the mountains. They hid in the woods and in caves—anywhere they felt they were safe.

Family members in the 1920s, photo taken at Apricale. My father is second seated boy from the left.

The Germans took over Apricale. When my parents returned to the village, they often had to hide. They had very little to eat and had to sneak out in fear to search for food. If they were caught, they would likely be shot.

One day, when my mom was home alone, she heard a knock at the door of their house. She thought it was her mother-in-law, so she opened the door. German soldiers were waiting behind it. My mom tried to keep them out, but the soldiers broke down the door and came into the house. They saw the barrel that was used for a latrine in the corner of the room and thought it was grappa, a strong Italian drink made from the fruit and stems of the grape plant that are left after winemaking. My parents tried to warn the soldiers, but they wouldn't listen. The barrel was pressurized, so when the Germans opened it, the barrel exploded in their faces. They were so angry they took my mom. They were going to shoot her, but their captain saw that she was going to have a baby and felt sorry for her. Before long, they let her go.

My mother and father survived WWII, and on June 26, 1945, my sister Roseanne was born in Apricale.

My father with his mother, Carlotta, on his right
and Camillo, his uncle, on his left.

Bordighera

By 1950, my family lived in Bordighera. My father was a mason, and my mother worked as a tailor. They could barely make a living. They had a small apartment for many years.

I was born on April 24, 1954, at a hospital in Sanremo.

Carlo Franco Martini.

When I was born, I had many health issues and almost died from malnutrition, possibly because of sensitivity to certain foods. I was eventually hospitalized. I still thank God I had a great doctor. Dr. Zecchi, a children's doctor who lived in town, saved my life. After I moved to America, I didn't see him for many years, not until I came back to Italy in the late '80s.

Me with Donald Duck.

When he saw me, Dr. Zecchi said, "Look at you now, my Carlone! You are tall and healthy and big as a bull!" In Italian "Carlone" means "big Carlo." It was wonderful to see him again.

Dr. Zecchi died not long after I saw him. He was a kind man. His ashes were thrown into the sea by Bordighera.

Me and my mom.

BORDIGHERA

Me and my mom.

My first communion.

The Journey of Carlo Martini

Me and my mom walking on a Sunday afternoon.

Me with my father on Bordighera Boardwalk.

First Voyage to America

At the age of two, in the summer of 1956, my mother and I took our first voyage across the Atlantic. My mother hoped that my luck in the United States was going to be better than in Italy.

We sailed off across the ocean on an Italian liner called *Andrea Doria*. I was so excited about coming to America. Until the worst happened. The luxury Italian liner *Andrea Doria* sank in a collision with the *S.S. Stockholm*, July 25, 1956. We were among the counted survivors that they rescued that night. Later in my life, my mom told me some of the details.

The *Andrea Doria* leaning to its starboard side,
not long before it sank.
Photo by Bob Wendlinger.

After that tragic night, when we arrived in the US at Long Island, New York, my grandfather and grandmother were there to pick us up. My mother and I were happy to finally step on American soil.

We stayed with my grandparents, who lived on a big farm in New Jersey. They had moved to the States from Varapodio, Calabria, in 1939.

Grandpa took me for rides into town in his 1955 Cadillac. I remember it looked like one of Elvis' cars. When we came back to New Jersey to stay years later in 1961, Grandpa took me on rides again, this time in a red pickup truck. We drove around the area selling peaches and pears.

The months went by fast, and we had to return to Italy so I could start kindergarten and my sister could continue her schooling. My mother went back to work. I didn't know then I would be returning to America several more times.

Back in Italy

I ALWAYS ENJOYED BEING PART OF THE LOCAL CHURCH CHORUS, AS well as being an altar boy. My feeling for music dated back to early childhood. I had music in my mind and in my heart every waking moment.

I recall listening to records from Italian and American artists such as Elvis, Tom Jones, Bobby Solo, Adriano Celentano, Little Tony, the Beatles and other rock-n-roll groups. Music took me over, and I sang every chance I got. I would sing in my family's apartment. The neighbors would often send me requests to sing songs. Other times, I sang so much people hit the wall to keep me quiet!

In the summer of 1962, when I was eight, my mother and I went for a walk on the boardwalk near the beach in Bordighera. Many people had gathered that evening. When we went to see the cause of all the commotion, we came upon a talent show for children. My mother said, "Let's sit here, son, and listen to the children singing."

A nice man approached us as we listened.

"Do you sing?" he asked me.

"Yes, he does," my mother said. I looked at my mom, surprised she answered for me. I felt very nervous.

The man continued speaking with my mom. A voice in my head said, "There is your chance. Go sing."

I turned to the man and said, "Yes. I'm ready."

"Good," he said. "What would you like to sing?"

"'Ciao, Ciao, Bambina.'" It is a Domenico Modugno song, a singer-songwriter star of Italy in the '60s.

"Well, let's go," the man said. I followed him to get me scheduled and learned I would be next. Many things came to my mind. *What will happen? I hope the audience will like me.*

The talent show that I was auditioning for, called the "Zecchino D'Oro," featured Mago Zurli as its host, an Italian celebrity. His program aired on Rai, national Italian television. The television team had chosen that afternoon to look for talent, and I happened to be there.

Mama and me on the way to the talent show.

I heard my name called. Mago Zurli said, "Come on, bambino. Come up and sing a song."

I walked to the front of the crowd.

"Are you ready?" he asked me.

"Yes," I said. "I'm ready."

"Well, there's the mic." He nodded to the stage. "Sing."

I felt a rush of energy taking over me. The people stared and listened intently. When I finished the song, the audience gave me an applause, and they started taking pictures. Mago Zurli came up and congratulated me. I left the stage to wait for the judge's decision.

A few minutes later, all the participants were called up on stage where we waited to hear what the judge would say. WOW! I had won second prize! I was so happy. All the people congratulated me. I thanked everyone as I left. I will never forget that evening.

My mother and I returned to our apartment. She was so happy and proud of me.

One day the man who worked at the bar in the lobby of our apartment building came upstairs to the third floor and knocked on our door. He told my mom that someone had called us. We didn't have a phone so we used the one downstairs at the bar. Mom went down to return the call and then came back to me.

"Son," she said, "they want you to be on TV." She had been speaking with the television studio. They got our telephone number from the people at the talent show.

"When, Mama?"

My mother smiled.

"In two weeks you will be on national TV."

I remember she took me to the shops to find a great little suit. She worried about my readiness.

The morning we left, we took the train to the city of Milano. Once we arrived at the station, we soon found the studio.

"Come on, let's go in." I felt nervous again. But Mom always made sure I stayed calm and ready to sing. We went through the doors.

The television studio surrounded us like a new world. We stood there gazing at everything around us. Then the organizer approached us. "You must be the little boy who sang a few months ago on the show for the talent search."

"Yes, sir, it's me!"

"Well, follow me, please."

As we entered a long hall that took us to our dressing room, the man said, "You will be on in twenty-five minutes." He showed us to a dressing room and walked quickly down the hall. He called back to us, "I'll come and get you, okay?"

"Thank you," I said.

I saw Mama looked worried.

"What's wrong?" I asked her.

"This is a big chance for you son, and there will be many people watching the show. Do not be nervous. Just sing."

"Don't worry. I'll be okay."

I heard my name called and went toward the stage. The studio lights were so bright it was hard to see. Everything appeared set to start. The show was live. I could see Mama smiling backstage near the curtains.

I sang a beautiful Italian song I had picked—"Ciao, ciao bambina."

When I finished, the clapping sounded greater than any I had ever heard . . . I had done it! I thanked the audience.

As I left the stage, I saw Mama in tears.

"Don't cry," I told her. "I did it, Mama. I did it."

"I am so proud of you," she said.

At the Movies as a Small Boy

I DIDN'T KNOW WHAT THE FUTURE WOULD BRING. I LOVED SHOW business. Music and singing quickly became a big part of my life.

There was a cinema in Bordighera that I went to when I was a child. Sometimes when I needed money for tickets to go to Cinema Olympia, I worked at the church around the corner and up the street. I did some chores and the priest gave me a little money, usually 500 lire. Back then, 500 lire was about seventy-five cents.

I loved going to the cinema to watch films—westerns, stories about Hercules, comedies, James Bond. I even watched *Cleopatra* from the box seats on the side of the room. It was a long movie to watch for a child. I especially loved watching Ann-Margret in *Bye Bye Birdie* and Jerry Lewis in all his films. I often dreamed of meeting them. That world of movies and celebrities fascinated me.

I went so often I made friends with a kind and gentle man who ran the projectors. I went every chance I had to speak to him and to learn more about how films worked. I watched as he threaded the film through the projector and then made it appear on the big screen of the theatre.

Cinema Olympia in Bordighera today.
It has been remodeled.

One day the man in the projection room said, "Why don't you try to be in some films?"

"How would I do that?" I asked.

"Well, go to Cinecitta and try out or write to them."

"I will."

I followed his words and mailed my photos to Cinecitta Studios in Rome. I had learned they were making a movie about Hercules, and I dreamed of being a part of it. I loved Hercules. I wanted to be just like Steve Reeves, the star of the film.

Meanwhile, I continued to attend every film, the theatre becoming a second home for me. I often stayed and watched the same movie over and over again. I learned many of the lines just like the actors on the screen. Sometimes after a film ended, I crawled underneath the seats, and when they turned off the lights for the start of the next film, I came out.

One day I received a letter from Rome. The recruiters invited me to audition as an extra for a Hercules film! I would actually go to Rome to the Cinecitta Studios. I was about eight years old at the time.

My mother and some friends of hers went to Rome with me. I recall a long line of kids around my age. I did not get to sing, but the audition went well. At the end of the next day, we would know the cast decisions.

That next day we received a call from the studio people. My mom told me I got the part! There were eighty kids who had auditioned and only twelve got picked. They wanted me on the set that following week. I was happy but nervous.

My scene took a few days to film. There I stood with Hercules. I was already such a big fan of his films. I had now appeared in one of his films in Rome. Too soon, I returned home with my mom, back to my everyday schedule of school.

Cinema Olympia still stands today, and I saw the kind man who told me to write to Cinecitta around the year 2000. He was still at Cinema Olympia working the projector. I told him that once when I was a child watching him work, he needed to fix the film for a Clint Eastwood movie. I watched as he cut out a piece and then carefully taped the film back together. When he finished, he gave me the piece. When I reminded him of this, he was surprised. He couldn't believe that I could remember it.

I can't remember his name, but I will never forget that kind man.

Meeting Elvis

When I was little growing up in Bordighera, I read something about an entertainer named "Elvis." I wanted to read more. As I did, I became very interested in his career and life.

I learned Elvis was in the army in Germany. A very young boy, I could not go to Germany on my own to see Elvis. However, I told my first cousin about him.

Rogero was in his early twenties. He was visiting us at the time in our town at my mom's home. I explained to him that I would like to see Elvis one day. Luckily, Elvis was his favorite singer!

"I have some friends near where he is stationed," he said. "Maybe we can see him."

"Oh, really? You're kidding!"

"No, it's true. I'll see what I can do. I'll let you know."

This was typical of my cousin. He always tried to make me happy. Weeks went by. Then one day Rogero came over to me and said, "Guess what?"

"What is it?"

"I think we can see Elvis."

"You mean it? When?"

"Soon," he said. "I spoke with my friends and they happen to know someone in the army there. They think maybe we can get to him." He was studying a map while he talked. "I'll take you there. We'll take the train."

My cousin had to get permission from my parents. Ordinarily, they would never let me go on such a trip. But they knew Rogero, a good person from a good family, so they agreed. I would be among family and would be looked after well.

So one morning we hopped on a train and went on our way. My cousin took great care of me. We changed trains a few times on the long trip. Our excitement increased as we neared Germany. We spoke of Elvis with great anticipation. We hoped to talk with him or at least see him. Finally, at the destination, I recall we took a taxi through town and to the home of the family and friends of my cousin. We were told to make ourselves welcome. We planned to stay for three or four days. I remember eating apple strudel for dessert.

The next day my cousin came to me with a smile on his face.

"Today is the day," my cousin said. "We will see Elvis."

I jumped up eagerly. "Are you sure?!"

"Well, we came all this way," he said, "and we are going to see him."

While he talked to his friends about the arrangements, I thought, *Will I really see Elvis?*

Rogero turned around and said, "We are going to see Elvis this very afternoon."

I recall it being a rainy day. And it was a bit cold. However, I was happy.

My cousin said, "Keep yourself covered up. I don't want you to get sick."

"Yes," I said. "Don't worry."

We went to meet some of my cousin's friends who would try to get us to Elvis. As we went on our way, I kept thinking: *Is this really happening?*

We all crowded into one car. As we approached the army post, I said, "Are you sure we will see Elvis?"

"We are here," Rogero said as we drove through the entrance of an army base. "We are going to see him."

It was 5:56 p.m. One of Rogero's friends got out of the car and talked to someone at the army post near the gate. Shortly after, he came back to us.

"In a few minutes, Elvis is leaving. We will wait here and try to see him."

Well, a few minutes were like days for me, especially with the rainy weather. However, I did not give up hope.

Then there he was! We were in a group of about twelve or thirteen, and some people started calling out to him.

"Elvis!"

I was speechless.

He rode up with some friends in a jeep. As he passed us, he waved. We all waved back.

"Ciao, Elvis! Hi!"

He stopped.

"What are you all doing in this weather?"

"We are here to see you," said one of my cousin's friends.

"Oh, thank you very much." He replied. He looked at everyone, including me, with concern.

"You better get warm." As he said that, he turned to a friend of my cousin who knew one of Elvis' army friends. "How about coming to the house this weekend?"

"Oh, that's great, Elvis! Thanks. We will, but my friends came a long way with this young boy, and they need to return soon, in a day or so."

"Well, you come over tomorrow. I have some time off, and we can get together."

"Okay, we'll be there."

After Elvis left, Rogero said, "You will see the house he is living in while he's stationed in Germany."

The following day we all went to Elvis' house. For me it was a dream come true. There were several people there. I stood next to the door.

Elvis answered the door in his army uniform. He greeted us with one hand while holding a sandwich in the other. He walked over to see his friend.

"How are you doing?" he asked us. "I'm glad you came to see me."

"Elvis, I'd like to introduce you to some of my friends. They have to leave and pick up the train in a few hours. They really love you, and they are big fans."

"Well, bring them over."

I looked up at Elvis and saw a great smile that I remember to this day. What a wonderful person he was! He said to Rogero and me, "Were you two at the army post yesterday?"

We didn't speak English, and we were trying to understand what he was saying. Luckily, my cousin knew a little bit. "Yes, that was us," he said.

"I worried about y'all, that you might get cold up there. Especially this little boy here." He smiled, shook my hand and said, "You stay out of the cold, okay?"

"Si, si!" I said.

We were there twenty-five minutes, I think, but it was the most memorable time of my life. When he said goodbye to us, he told us to take care.

"If you're ever in America one day, come to Graceland and visit me."

Unfortunately, we had to go back to Italy. So we said our goodbyes. In fact, we needed to get to the train station before we missed the departure, but we did not want to leave. We wanted to stay with Elvis.

I became even more of a fan of Elvis as the years went by. The nice man from Memphis. I followed his career when I arrived in the USA in 1966. He became a part of my life, like family. I am sure that is true for many fans.

I saw his NBC Comeback Special in 1968 with his black leather jumpsuit and his red guitar.

Rogero stands behind older family members, photo taken in Apricale in late '70s.

My First Autograph

My DREAM TO MEET CELEBRITIES STARTED AT AN EARLY AGE IN Italy. I was ten years old when I saw Haley Mills and became a big fan of hers. I still am today.

I decided to write to her in California. A few months later, I received a photo of her, which I still have on my living room wall. My dream to meet her personally remained, but I never had the chance. I wrote to her again several years ago at her address in England. It was so nice of her to write to me in return and send an updated signed photo, which I will cherish forever.

My dream of meeting the stars was never over. The photos I gathered expanded into a significant collection. I still hope to meet her one day.

 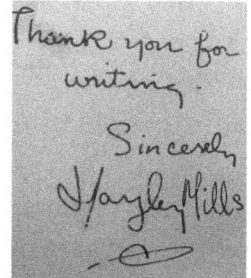 

Picture on left is Haley as she appears in Walt Disney's *Summer Magic*. She sent the photo on the right from England.

My Return to America

I TRAVELED MORE TIMES WITH MY PARENTS ACROSS THE GRAND Atlantic Ocean on many Italian ocean liners, including *Raffaello, Leonardo da Vinci, Cristoforo Columbo* and *Michelangelo*. These were very big passenger ships. Despite my tendency for seasickness, I loved the voyages and the return to the states to visit my relatives in New Jersey.

After a year back in Italy, my older sister left for America alone. She went to stay with family in New Jersey. My parents and I remained in Italy for two more years, and then in 1966, at the age of twelve, I moved to America with my father and mother to live in New Jersey. That seven-day trip would be my last on a ship.

We stopped at Gibraltar and the Canary Islands and then went straight to the United States. I found the trip rough, as did my mom and, I am sure, others who suffered seasickness. Dad used to be a sailor in the Italian Navy, so he did not find the sea distressing. Mom and I could not wait to arrive in America.

The day before our arrival, the sea seemed a bit calmer. I remember my mom looking at the ocean and with a big smile saying, "Son . . . we are almost there." We breathed in the ocean breeze.

"That's wonderful, Mama," I said.

"Soon we will be home, son." She stared out over the water toward our destination.

My father just walked around the deck of the ship and looked at the ocean.

The next day we had to get ready for our arrival. I remember a beautiful sunset that evening.

In the morning, seagulls were flying around the ship and we could see the New York port and the buildings in the distance. Little ships approached to anchor us in. I looked to my left and saw one of the most beautiful sights I had ever seen . . . the Statue of Liberty.

We entered the port at the Verrazano Bridge. I remember my mother holding onto me and looking at all the scenery as the ship made port. Everyone prepared to disembark. Among the hundreds of people, some were just travelers who were visiting the city, and some were ready to meet their families for the very first time.

We followed the line through customs. People all around us claimed their luggage. As we passed through the customs security, we heard far to our left our names being called out.

"Mom! Mom!"

My sister Roseanne, who had been living on my grandfather's farm, ran to us. She had accompanied my grandparents and other friends who had come to meet us. They hugged us and immediately went to get our luggage and trunk. Finally, I was in America to stay.

Englishtown, New Jersey

We drove away from the port on a big highway toward northern New Jersey. For a short while, we went to live in Englishtown where my sister had moved with her husband. She had met him while living with my uncle.

After a week or so, I started middle school in the center of Englishtown, but I was only there for a few months.

I did not speak a word of English and did not understand some things in life, like taking the school bus. In Italy, I always walked to school. However, bus riding became lots of fun, an adventure for me, a new frontier.

I made friends almost immediately. I heard a girl playing violin one day in the schoolyard. I can't remember her name, but I can still remember her face and the color of her hair. Reddish brown hair. She was about my age, or close to it. I just could not stop listening to her wonderful music. Soon, she noticed me watching her.

"Do you like my violin playing?" she asked.

I really didn't understand what she said, so I said, "Yes, yes!"

But it came out in Italian.

"Si, si!"

She understood and tried to explain the violin to me. She knew a bit of Spanish, so in a few days we were able to understand one another. Italian and Spanish are very similar. We became great friends.

Sometimes we stood under a tree in the schoolyard while she played the violin for me. She always played classical music.

She looked out for me whenever we were together. She made sure I went back home on the right bus after school. The same bus she rode. She was the only one who would sit next to me.

One day my friend came by my house with a beautiful gift: a little puppy.

"Oh, it's beautiful," I said. "Thank you so much!"

My dog, Pucci, is the little one on the right.

She smiled. "She will be your friend."

"Oh, thank you so much . . ." I had no words to describe what I was feeling.

I had never had a dog before, so this was a very special gift. I named her "Pucci."

My new puppy and I—we became good buddies! She always waited for me after school at the spot where the bus would bring me home at 4:15 p.m. We had a great time in the fields near the house. My sister had a horse named Tina. At times, when I rode Tina around, my little dog followed us everywhere. I think she always worried about me when I rode.

Tina and me.

The first Christmas with my family in America.

For several weeks, Mom and Dad tried to find a place nearby, but it was difficult because Dad couldn't find a job. One day they decided we needed to move about thirty miles away to where he had found work.

"Mama!" I said. "That means I have to change schools!"

"I'm sorry, son," she replied. "We have no choice."

I had to start over again, leaving my friend from school behind and all the things I had begun to get used to. I was so unhappy.

A week before we left, when I returned home from school, my dog was not waiting for me. *Why is she not here?* Afraid, I looked all over for her.

When my mom saw me, she called to me. "Son! I have to tell you something very sad."

"What, Mama?"

"Pucci passed away today when you were in school."

"Oh, no!" I didn't want to believe it. I started running everywhere, trying to find her in the fields, calling her name. But she did not come to me.

My mom tried to calm me. "Son. I know you loved that dog. I know she was dear to you, but she's gone."

"How, Mama, how?"

"Well, she ran off the property into the road, and a car ran over her."

"No . . . I want to see my dog!"

"It's not a good idea, son!" But I did. We went to the dog doctor. He helped me say goodbye to her, and I made sure she had a good burial. She was gone. To this day, she is still in my heart.

I said goodbye to my dear friend from school a few days before we left. We met in the afternoon in the schoolyard at our usual place under the tree where I had first heard her playing the violin. She was upset that I had to leave, and she became even more upset when I told her about my dog.

She cried as we said our goodbyes. I knew I would never see her again.

I will always have fond memories of her. Who knows, maybe she is playing violin in a great orchestra somewhere.

My First School

Manalapan-Englishtown Middle School. 1966.

Jamesburg, New Jersey

We packed all our things into a U-Haul truck the following week, and we moved to a new town called Jamesburg, New Jersey. It was 1967.

We settled in an apartment on Bucklew Avenue near the school and near some little shops. To meet our needs, my father took a job as a mason. Mom worked in a factory nearby preparing boxes for shipping, and I attended school.

My first day at the John F. Kennedy Elementary School, I still did not speak great English. I found the adjustment hard. A very nice teacher, Mrs. Ligrend, tried to teach me the language. Another teacher, Mrs. Toth, in the same manner as the teacher at my prior school, hung little cards on different objects, such as CHAIR, SEAT and WINDOW. Another teacher, a substitute, also helped teach me English. Her daughter Pamela was in my class and became my friend until middle school.

As the year went by, my English became better and better. I could finally communicate with my friends and my teachers. I would attend John F. Kennedy Elementary until it was time to go to high school.

While I was in middle school, a group of people did not like me. They felt the need to bully me all the time.

Jamesburg, New Jersey

A couple of the bullies beat me up several times, usually when I returned to my apartment after school. I had to cross the railroad tracks, and there were three to five people usually waiting on me, and then WAMO! I tried to go a different route, but they still waited for me.

I often arrived home with black eyes and bleeding lips. It overwhelmed me. Mama was worried. She went to the principal but could not put a stop to it because it happened after school.

Finally, I received some help one day. An exchange student from Texas asked me, "What's wrong?" He saw my cut lip and the bruises on my neck. Thinking back, I believe his name was Roy.

"Well . . . ah . . . I am getting beat up a lot!"

"Yeah? Who?"

I told him.

"Oh, don't worry. You just aren't defending yourself. Well . . . I'll take care of it."

Well, that nice friend became like a bodyguard to me. The bullies never bothered me again.

When he left a year before we finished middle school, he said, "You should learn the martial arts. They'll help you someday."

I took his advice and signed up for a self-defense program in high school.

One day in 1968, we received a telephone call with bad news. Grandpa had died. I recall I was watching TV when we got the news. Grandpa was gone! He was the first person close to me who had died. My mom's father. She grieved for a long time.

I graduated from middle school in 1969. We decided to stay in the area for a little while longer.

At the end of summer in August 1969, we left Jamesburg to go to South River, several miles away. There we lived in a small house at 22 Appleby Avenue in a quiet neighborhood. My father continued working as a bricklayer, and Mom worked at times as a tailor. My father turned the garage in the basement into a living room.

I was in the 9th grade in high school. For the first year, I had to take the school bus. It took me downtown where the high school was located.

On my second year I was able to walk to school. South River High School that I attended for the last three years was only fifteen minutes up and down the hill, near the church, just around the corner. The school had achieved fame because some of the students who attended in the late '60s had become football stars! These players included Joe Theisman, Kevin Hill and Drew Pearson.

During my high school days, I worked part-time at the Pancake House in East Brunswick. I rode my bike to work about one mile or so . . . Mr. Morgan, the manager, hired me as dishwasher and at times as busboy.

One day I was cleaning with my broom and decided to use it as a guitar. I started singing in the kitchen . . .

I heard a voice say, "Mr. Martini you are here to work, not to sing."

"But, Mr. Morgan, I . . . just couldn't help it."

"Please return to work . . ."

"Yes, sir," I said.

In the following few days I was fired from the Pancake House.

"I hate to let you go," he told me, "but you really need to be in show business."

I was very surprised by his comments and thanked him for his compliments. "Pick up your check on Friday," he said.

I told him, "One day I will come back when I have appeared on television . . ." And I did.

My first car, a Ford Galaxy, at the age of seventeen.

When I arrived at South River across town, it seemed like a new world. I had to get used to everything, but I quickly started making friends.

My dream of show business always stayed in my mind, and at times I just dreamed away!

I signed up for chorus classes. I felt that would help me a lot with my singing. My chorus teacher, always kind and helpful, said, "Why don't you sing for the school assembly one day?"

"Ah, I don't know if I could," I told her. I was nervous.

"You will be fine. Trust me!"

Sometimes the entire chorus sang for the school, and when I sang among others, I found it easier. I looked at all the students around me and in the seats in the audience and thought, Why not? Maybe I can do it. So I did.

I sang a song called "More," the theme from *Mondo Cane.* As I finished, I was afraid everyone would leave, but instead I heard great applause. Deep inside me, I knew then I could look to the future as a singer.

A few weeks went by, and I soon became used to the school and the town of South River. I liked living there, going downtown to walk around and look at shops. I went into a music shop several times where I could just sit and listen to people talking about music and playing instruments.

My first day at school I had to register for classes and get my books. I soon learned my way to my classes and could remember my teachers' names. I had chorus classes again, of course. I even signed up for drama classes to be in the school play!

I really enjoyed the chorus classes. For some odd reason, my teacher Mrs. Prentiss never remembered my name. She always referred to me by the color of my sweater because of my style of clothes—a bit different from the others. More colorful.

"Yellow Sweater, come up and sing," she would say. She liked the way I sang. "You have potential. Remember that! Work on it, and you will be successful."

"Thank you," I told her. "I will remember that."

I enjoyed the drama classes, especially the parts in the various plays. Mr. Nowack, the director of the plays, said, "Carlo, you have talent and determination. That's what it takes, and you have it."

Acting felt natural to me, and I learned how to do it quickly. One of the first high school plays in 1971 was *How to Succeed in Business without Really Trying*. My role was an office worker, an extra. In 1973, I got a role as one of the Gallant Knights in *Camelot*. We dressed in medieval clothes with swords. Although I loved to participate in the plays, my singing always came first.

The Image Players
I'm in the back row, a little left of the middle,
mostly hidden behind the young man in the suit. The director,
George Nowack, is seated fifth from the left in the first row.

Many of the drama classes happened after school. By the time I finished and arrived home, it was time for dinner. After I ate, I felt very tired and still had homework to do. Sometimes I would fall asleep on my books in my room.

Me as Gallant Knight in *Camelot*.

Mom told me I needed to concentrate more on my studies than on acting. "You must study," she said. "You are involved too much after school. With the drama class, you don't have much time to work, son!"

"Yes, Mama, I know. But I like it."

"Well," she said, "maybe you can be involved a few days a week . . . but not every day."

"Okay, Mama."

I always listen to my mom, and I believe she was right this time. So I gave it up except for two times a week. When I did drama classes every day, my attention stayed on show business. I could not shake it out of my head. Anything from singing to acting. Films, the music business, photo collections of celebrities—it got the best of me. During my classes, I dreamed away, sitting at my desk and looking out the window, my head always in the clouds because I was always dreaming about show business and stardom, not concentrating on my homework.

One of my teachers spotted me not paying attention. I was looking out the window in a trance. He came up to my desk.

"Mr. Martini," he said.

Looking up at him, swallowing hard, I smiled. "Yes sir?"

"Are you dreaming of Hollywood again?"

"Oh, no, sir. I'm not." But I was. I didn't want to let him know that was exactly what I was doing.

"You better concentrate on your homework, and don't drift away."

"Yes, sir."

Sometimes I serenaded the girls in the hallway. One time while I was singing to several girls, I had forgotten I had to be in class. The principal had come up behind me and was listening to me sing "We've Only Just Begun" by The Carpenters.

As I finished the song, I heard a voice behind me. "Mr. Carlo Martini, you better stop serenading the girls and return to class."

When I heard that voice, I knew it could only be one person . . . the principal. Mr. Alfred E. Losiewicz.

"Mr. Martini . . ."

"Yes, sir?"

"Are you supposed to be in class?"

"Ah . . . oh, yeah."

"Don't let me catch you again."

"No, sir, I won't."

Mr. Losiewicz was walking away, but then he suddenly stopped and turned around. "Well you do sing well, I have to say."

That was so nice to hear. It made me smile.

"But get back to class."

I returned to class.

As I walked through the hall, I was thinking, Wow, just imagine if I can get everyone's attention when I sing and be in front of an audience. That would be great!

Sometimes I sat in the auditorium during lunch break and dreamed away. I dreamed about singing in front of an audience in my school auditorium and girls screaming like they did for Elvis. Perhaps it was only a dream, a vision that lasted a few minutes, but I always knew a dream comes true if you believe in it and do everything you can to make it happen.

Even if other people discourage me, I have always picked myself up. I do not let them bother me. But it is not always so easy . . .

. . .

Going to school was hard for me at times because I was always in the dream world, far, far away from earth. However, I tried to get good grades.

I was even involved in sports. Wrestling was my favorite, and I also liked baseball. The coach, Mr. Dudra, sometimes said, "You have a future in those sports." I really did not know what I was doing, but once in baseball everyone wanted me on their team. They saw that I would hit balls out of the field. When the coach saw me do this, he told me I should go out for baseball. However, singing was the number one thought on my mind.

Getting the attention of the girls also motivated me to play sports. Nevertheless, as much as I liked playing sports, my dream remained show business.

Wrestling and playing baseball attracted attention but not dates. I tried to find a girlfriend in high school but had no luck for some reason. Maybe they found me a bit different from the others.

However, soon I would show them all what I could do.

Talent Show at Middlesex County Fair

I DECIDED TO PARTICIPATE IN A TALENT SHOW AT A COUNTY FAIR IN 1972. I selected a love song for my performance.

One of the most beautiful girls I had ever seen stood next to me in line: number seven. She looked angelic with beautiful blue eyes and black hair.

"What are you going to do?" she asked.
"I'll be singing."
"Oh, that's great!"
"What about you?" I asked her.
"I will be dancing to a jazz number."
"Wonderful!" I said. "What's your name?"
"Ellen."
"Hi, Ellen. My name is Carlo."

Ellen danced great that evening. After her performance, we waited for the judge's decision. Finally, he announced that I won second place and a trumpet player, third. Ellen won the first prize! I felt so happy for her. When she walked on stage for her prize, she turned around and smiled at me. I knew she would be my friend.

That night, as I said goodbye to Ellen, I asked for her number, not knowing if I would ever see her again. I waited two weeks and then spoke with her on the phone about her winning and her future dreams.

. . .

Ellen was a senior in a high school several miles from me in Edison, New Jersey. A junior, I would not graduate for another year. She did not mind being my friend. She loved to hear the stories about my dreams and goals.

We talked a lot after that, but I wanted to see her again. Then one day, she called me. I remember I was upstairs in the kitchen. "Would you like to come over to the house?" she asked.

"Yeah, sure," I said. "I would love to, but I don't have my car yet."

"Don't worry. I'll pick you up, okay?"

"I'll be waiting."

She drove up in a yellow 1970 Mustang. *This is not a dream,* I told myself.

We went for a ride and then to her house. Her mom was a very kind woman. We all sat around talking about things like show business. Ellen wanted to open a dance school.

"That's great," I said.

"What are your goals?" she asked.

"I want to be someone in show business."

"You have the potential and talent to make it."

"What about you signing up for a beauty pageant?" I asked.

"Oh, I couldn't do that."

"You're beautiful and talented. You would win, trust me."

When I said this, Ellen paused and her eyes opened wide. She was surprised by what I'd said. Then she smiled. "Oh, Carlo, I don't know."

"Well, think about it."

"Okay."

Talent Show at Middlesex County Fair

As she drove me home that day, we talked a little more about the pageant. As I said goodbye, she kissed me on the cheek.

I hoped she would agree to my idea.

A week later, I heard of a pageant for the county! *There is her chance,* I thought. *I must try to sign her up.* However, I could not enroll her without her permission. When I called to convince her, she said, "Yes."

I just knew good things would happen. I signed her up and gave the people in charge of the event a photo of her.

Although we had started dating before the pageant and everyone knew I had a girlfriend, they didn't know she would be in the county event.

The show was at my favorite place in school: the auditorium. I went there sometimes on my own. At those times, I sat on the bleachers and looked at the empty stage and dreamed. The evening of the pageant, the crowd packed the large room. My family and Ellen's family sat in the same row. I excused myself. "I need to be backstage with Ellen," I told them. "She may need me."

When I went backstage, I saw her. Clearly the most beautiful person there.

Ellen looked at me and smiled. "Hi," she said.

"Are you okay, Ellen?"

"Yes, just a bit nervous."

"You will be fine. Just go on, you're the best." She was stretching and holding onto my shoulder for balance. I loved that everyone was looking at us, noticing she was with me. I gave her a good luck kiss and walked toward my seat.

"Hey, Carlo," I heard my name and turned around. One of my classmates called, "Who is the pretty girl you're with? She's beautiful. You like her?"

41

"Yes, she's my girlfriend."

"Oh . . . really?" He froze at my response.

"Yes, she will win," I said. "I need to return to my seat now. Bye."

That night she danced better than I had ever seen her do. She was a true beauty. The judges were ready to give out their decision. I prayed and hoped she would win. Her mom held my arm. "Don't worry." I told her. "She will be fine."

The moment came, and the emcee called her name. She had won the pageant! Ellen was Miss Middlesex County. Photographers and other people ran toward her to get a photo and autograph. Ellen became a local celebrity that very evening.

As I watched her on stage, it reminded me of Hollywood stars with photographers all around. Ellen posed for the photos. I noticed she was looking for me. I know she wanted me to be next to her.

When I went backstage, she came up to me and said, "I can't believe I won!"

"I said you would win."

Later that night we said goodbye and went our separate ways.

I called her the next day. She was happy. "I still cannot believe I won. Everyone at school is congratulating me."

"That's great. I'm happy for you."

"What about you?" she asked me.

"Well, everybody knows I'm dating you. They stop me in the halls and ask how you're doing."

"Wow . . . okay, I'll talk to you later."

It felt wonderful being her friend.

Weeks and months went by. We dated seldom because she had many obligations to fulfill.

One day she called. "I'm getting too much publicity. I can't even go to the grocery store without someone stopping me."

"Ah, it must be a great feeling."

"It is."

I wondered if she would sign up for Miss New Jersey. She did and took runner-up. She called me right away to tell me. Two weeks after the state pageant, she came by my house in South River. She brought Miss Virginia with her. Oh, man! I could hardly believe I was in the company of not only runner-up Miss New Jersey, but also Miss Virginia . . .

After that visit, I never saw her or heard from her again. My memories of that beautiful young woman will always remain in my heart.

Brotherhood of Magicians Ring 200

IN 1971, DURING MY YEARS IN HIGH SCHOOL IN SOUTH RIVER, New Jersey, I became interested in watching magicians perform. I wanted to know how they made things disappear and how they made a rabbit come out of a hat.

Me at age sixteen as a magician's assistant
with Art and Ellen Swan in their show *Raydini and Company*.

I had a neighbor named Don, a school friend, who was a magician. He had performed the lead role in the play with me, *How to Succeed in Business without Really Tying*. I went over to his house sometimes to get him to show me magic.

One day at Don's house, he told me he knew of a magician who needed an assistant.

"When can I meet him?" I asked.

"I will speak to him soon and introduce you."

A few weeks went by, then one day he called me. "I can take you to meet the magician today."

We drove to New Brunswick, not far from where I lived, and I met Mr. Swan. We developed a friendship, and I became his assistant. I went over to his apartment several days a week for two weeks to learn the act. I found it very interesting. I helped him with a lot of shows—a New Years Eve event, magic conventions and many more. I was sixteen at the time. Working with his show, *Raydini and Company*, I learned magic tricks of the trade, from rabbit appearances to disappearing cards. I went a little further, working on my own, to learn the Harry Houdini escape tricks.

This is me doing one of the magic acts on my own.

One day Mr. Swan invited me to a meeting of local magicians in the basement of a nearby church in New Brunswick. Mr. Swan always came to pick me up for these meetings, held the first Tuesday of every month. He introduced me to many magicians who welcomed me like part of a family. The meetings consisted of speeches and people showing their magic tricks.

Sometimes I did a demonstration. The magicians all seemed to like what I did. They pointed out anything wrong with particular tricks and how to do them right. I learned from my mistakes—all the magicians helped. After a few months, they invited me to join "The Brotherhood of Magicians Ring 200."

David Copperfield and me, 2003.

After a year passed, a sixteen-year-old boy from the nearby town of Metuchen, who went by the name Davino, showed me some of his tricks when he visited me at my home in South River. He later became the renowned David Copperfield. Davino had a rabbit and bird disappearing act he sold to me for twenty-five bucks. We became very good friends.

We sat together in the monthly meetings. Davino always said he would be famous one day. I wished him the best. I liked Davino's real name and encouraged him to use it. I told him about my dreams of becoming a famous singer and actor. He said we needed a magic trick to make it all happen.

Little did I know he would become a world-famous magician. In 2003, I saw him in New Jersey, and we rekindled our friendship. I saved many articles about him from the media.

The National Book of Magicians added my name in the early '70s. I did several shows on my own and even sang in them, billed as the singing magician. I appeared live in 1972 on the CBS *John Bartholomew Tucker Show*. I was doing a Houdini trick in front of the New York Pan Am Building. The show was aired everywhere in America. When I returned to South River and school, I had become a local celebrity.

I continued my magic shows and assisting Mr. Swan. My last appearance was an assistant at a magician convention. The act was great.

The evening after our act, Mr. Swan and I sat in the audience in the darkness while other magicians performed. When the lights were dimmed, we could not see who was sitting close to us. The emcee announced there was a celebrity in the house, and the spotlight aimed toward me. Who is sitting near me? I thought. The emcee then told us Muhammad Ali was in the audience. He sat only two chairs away from me! He stood up and waved to everyone. He prided himself in being a big fan of magic. The emcee called him to join him on stage, and as he made his way to the stage, he tripped, and I grabbed him to keep him from falling. He seemed very grateful.

When he returned to his seat, he started speaking to reporters and sat down right next to me. We talked a little, and he told me how much he loved magic. I told him I loved to sing.

He said, "You are a champ and don't ever give up, no matter what is in front of you. You must keep your chin up and fight to the top."

I thanked him for his kind words. I will never forget his encouragement and strength.

During my high school days, I continued looking for opportunities to speak to stars and request photos.

My encounters included Peter Lupus, from *Mission Impossible*, Jackie Coogan who played Uncle Fester from *The Adams Family* and also some sport figures, including Mario Andretti, Hulk Hogan, Joe Theisman and Mohammed Ali.

Peter Lupus and I at Woodbridge Mall in New Jersey, fall of 1973.

Peter Lupus and I at a gym in Florida in 1976.

My meetings with the stars increased in 1973, when I moved with my family to the east coast of Florida.

The Move to Florida

It was September 3, 1973, and my family decided to move to Port St. Lucie on Southeast Calmosa Drive.

It took us a few days to arrive in Florida in a U-Haul Truck. That evening I recall we were all very tired and settled in the new house that my father had bought. It was a great brick home sitting on the corner looking over a river.

Two weeks went by and my father took on a new job working for General Development Constructions in Port St. Lucie. I worked with him for a few months. The work "was not my cup of tea." In addition, I took up a job at the Port St. Lucie Hilton as a busboy and waiter.

I got the chance to meet all kinds of people. However, my dream was always to entertain as a singer . . .

One evening I went to listen to a band that was playing at the lounge in the Hilton. It was a three-piece band with a nice sound. I went to introduce myself to them and spoke with the leader.

"Hi. My name is Carlo Martini. I really like your music style."

"Thanks," he said. "My name is Ossie Wright Jr. Nice to meet you."

As we spoke, I told him I sang and where I was from.

"We're looking for a front man to sing. What kind of music you sing?"

"Well," I said, "I can sing anything from Elvis to Sinatra to Italian music."

"Great man! Can you come to the house next week, and we can rehearse with the band?"

"Sure, Ossie!"

I could not believe it. I was going to audition with his band . . .

"Okay," he said. "I'll see you."

"Okay, bye, Ossie."

The following week I got together with his band. They liked me. I sang with them, doing shows and weddings, private parties, hotels and yacht clubs in Vero Beach, Florida.

The last time I saw Ossie was in 1979, but we stayed great friends and kept in touch until the day he passed away on April 21, 2013, three days before my birthday.

Ossie had won several jazz music awards for his piano playing.

I also met Claude Atkins at Port St. Lucie during the time I met Ossie Wright.

Ossie Wright Jr, in memoriam, permission for the photo received from from his son, Paul Wright.

Nashville

In March 1974, I went from Port St. Lucie to Orlando for an audition. A producer from Nashville wanted new talent, so I made an appointment to try out.

On arrival in Orlando, I went directly to the producer's office. We spoke of a future recording opportunity in Nashville and the songs that would fit me.

I traveled to Orlando several times after that and finally met a man by the name of Bill Walker. He was arranger and producer for many television country specials, such as the *Johnny Cash Show*. He heard my voice and really liked me.

"You sound great," he said. "I'll give you two songs to learn for the month, and then we'll schedule you to come to Nashville."

"Whoa! Really?" I was surprised and excited. "Well, thanks. I will learn them as soon as I get home." As I left, I thought, *I am actually going to Nashville . . .*

Mr. Walker scheduled me to go a month later, the first week of April. Spring arrived and I prepared to leave. I had received a call and letter telling me when to be at the recording studio. Thrilled, I thought, *The big time is here!*

I left the next day from the airport in West Palm Beach and arrived at my destination in the late afternoon. This was my first time ever in Nashville, the city of country music legends. The day seemed especially beautiful.

I went to the front of the airport and immediately took a taxi to The Hall of Fame, my hotel located near Music Square Road.

After I checked in and went to settle in my room, I found out Elvis stayed in the hotel when he used to record in Nashville. *I am actually staying in the place my idol stayed in . . .*

Mama always worried about me, so I phoned her to let her know I had arrived safely and proceeded to prepare for the next day's recording session. I went over my songs repeatedly. I thought, *Maybe Elvis did the same thing in this very room!*

The next morning I arose at 7:25 a.m., worried. I hoped all would turn out great. I called the studio from my room and told them I would be there soon. I was nervous. This would be my first time in a recording studio.

I left the hotel, my hands and legs shaking, and decided to walk there instead of taking a taxi. That could help my tension. The studio was not far from the hotel. It was located on Music Square Road among the other recording studios and other record companies.

Suddenly, there it was! It took me a little while to walk toward it. I arrived around 1:00 p.m.

When I reached the building, I told myself, *Take a deep breath and just go inside.*

I opened the doors. Oh my! I saw everyone from the producer to the technicians, all staring at me.

"Hey Carlo! How's it going?"

"Oh, just fine."

Everybody was busy in the studio getting the equipment ready. I smiled. It felt good. When it looked like everything was set up, I asked, "Everybody ready?"

"Yep, we are whenever you are!" By then it was 1:20 p.m.

We went immediately to work. They gave me earmuffs and put me in a booth next to a mic. While they performed the starting setup, a strange feeling came over me, like a group of butterflies inside me. However, I could not give up! *You are here,* I thought to myself. *You are here, do not give up!*

They gave me a signal to start. When I heard the music, something took over me. I did not feel nervous anymore. Those butterflies vanished . . . amazing! I sang "I'm Only Human" and "Misery Loves Company."

We required several takes—five to be exact. It was perfect. *I did it!* I thought to myself

The press came over to take a photo for the Nashville paper. I looked at the clock. It was 6:58 p.m. The session was over. Everyone congratulated me and said goodnight.

I felt a sense of ease and felt good about my recording. I had achieved something I had always dreamed of doing.

As everyone was leaving, the producer said, "Hey, Carlo! I'll drive you back to the hotel. You did great!"

"Thanks. I hoped you'd like it."

"Yeah, I sure did. Soon we'll make the record and try to have a radio station play it."

"Really? My voice will be on the radio?" I had been on the radio before for interviews and occasional songs, but not with formally recorded music. I had no words. Happiness filled me, and energy flowed through my body.

53

"So, do you want me to drive you back to your hotel?"

"Ah, no, no, I'm fine. I'm going to walk there."

"Okay," he said. "Be careful. Take care. I will be in touch!"

I walked through the city and thought about the recording session. I could not believe all went so well at the studio. I celebrated that evening. I went out to a great restaurant in the city of Nashville, and after I ate, I visited some clubs. One was Boots Randolph's.

A great band was playing there. I stayed and listened for a few hours. I introduced myself to some band members around 11 p.m. When they took a break, I told them who I was, where I was from and that I had just recorded a record that day for the first time. They liked my story and asked me to sing with them.

"What would you like to sing?" the guitarist asked.

"'For the Good Times.'" It was a song Ray Price made famous.

"Oh, we like his music too," the person in charge of the band said. "You're on." They called me up a few minutes later.

I was on with a great band of musicians. It felt like we had practiced for weeks even though it was the first time we performed together. The people applauded and cheered.

"Do one more," the leader said. I sang, "Make the World Go Away." Once more, there was applause. It was a great feeling.

The guitarist grabbed the mic and said, "This young man just recorded a record today. Remember his name when his song comes out: CARLO MARTINI!" I was touched and thanked him for the promotion.

A few people came up to congratulate me as I was leaving the stage. They wanted to know when the record would come out. It was a great moment. I thought, *I just wanted to go out, celebrate and visit a nightclub . . . I had no idea it would turn out like this. This is what I call a celebration!*

As I went to sit down, there was a young woman at the corner of the bar, speaking about music with several people. One of her friends came to me and said, "You sounded great up there."

"Thank you, sir!"

"Would you like to join us?"

"Sure, thanks."

As I did, they introduced me to a very beautiful young woman. I did not know who she was. We spoke for several minutes, and she seemed to like my company. I liked her company as well.

After a while, a few people asked her to sign photos. She got up to meet them. While she was holding a photo and signing it, she turned to me and said, "This is part of being successful." As I smiled at her, I had no idea she was important in country music. She came back to the bar, sat next to me and smiled.

"Must be great to sign photos," I said.

"Yes, it's wonderful when people love you like that."

After I talked to her some more, I realized she was Tanya Tucker. Oh, my God! I am sitting with Tanya Tucker! "I'm so sorry I didn't recognize you sooner," I told her.

"That's okay." She smiled again. "Carlo, you have to keep the faith and determination to make it. You'll find in time you want to give up, but you must stand tall and keep going."

"Thank you. I love your voice and music," I said. She returned the compliment.

It was late. I needed to return to the hotel. I had to catch an early flight. I thanked her, and she gave me a big hug and kiss.

"Bye, Tanya. I'll see you one day soon!" I would be making other trips to Nashville.

Once back in Florida, I returned to my regular working days and weekend singing while deep in the back of my mind I would always be thinking about my recording and what would happen with it.

Weeks passed with no response from Nashville.

One day, country singer Jimmy Dickens came to town. I had heard about him in Nashville, so I wanted to meet him. And I did!

That evening he appeared at The Armory. I saw him there signing photos and went up to him and introduced myself.

"Mr. Dickens. Hi, my name is Carlo."

"Hi. How are you?"

"I just returned from Nashville where I did a recording, and soon I'll have my 45 single."

"Oh, that's great. I'm going to perform soon. Would you like to sing before I come on?"

"Mr. Dickens, that would be great!"

"Come here for a second. Let me hear what you will sing."

I sang for a few seconds. Apparently he liked my voice.

"Okay, son, you're on."

As the emcee introduced me, Mr. Dickens stood on the right side of the stage, looking and listening. I did a few songs that evening, including "Make the World Go away" and "Help Me Make It Through the Night." The audience applauded vigorously. Jimmy came up and said, "Give a great hand for this young boy! He sounded great!"

I shook his hand. "Thank you," I said. I waved to everyone and stepped off the stage.

That evening seemed like magic. A well-known promoter of country music was in the audience and had heard me sing. He came up and introduced himself.

"I'd like you to open up for some concerts in the area. Would you be interested?" He liked what he had heard. I was pleased with myself.

"Yes, sir!"

"Okay, here's my card. Call me in a day or two. We'll talk."

I did that and several opportunities arose for me. I opened for Mel Tillis, Roy Clark, Hank Snow, Carl Smith and one more time for Jimmy Dickens. These appearances gave me a new start in a new direction.

Mel Tillis in a 1976 show where I opened for him.

I opened for several other country stars, such as Tom T. Hall and Jim Ed Brown, but also for celebrities like Sammy Davis Jr., comedian London Lee, comedian Pat Cooper and actor Telly Savalas.

I traveled several times to Nashville to make appearances. My 45 single came out and aired in some states—that was a great moment in my life. I was surrounded by happiness and magic. I went back and recorded a second single with the songs "I Can See Forever in Your Eyes" by Don King, and "Sweet Tomorrow" by Dean Shek.

This is Carl Smith.
He was with Mel Tillis when I opened for them.

I sang one evening in one of the Nashville clubs with another wonderful woman who invited me to step on stage. Her name was K.T. Olsin.

"You have lots of potential there, keep up the good work," she said.

Author with London Lee in Miami Beach 1975 at the Diplomat Hotel.

Author with London Lee in Florida a year before he passed away in 2015.

Sammy Davis Jr.

I WENT TO MIAMI BEACH IN 1973 WHEN I LEARNED SAMMY DAVIS Jr., was going to perform in one of the hotels on Collins Avenue. I was excited to meet him since I had been a longtime fan of his and the Rat Pack. I traveled one hour and forty-five minutes by bus from my home in Port St. Lucie and arrived in Miami with my camera and a little money, knowing I would be returning the same day. I was not certain I would be able to see Sammy.

When I arrived at the bus terminal in Miami, I immediately went to the Diplomat Hotel where he was going to perform. I asked when the show would start and what time Sammy would be arriving. Everyone had different answers.

I waited there patiently. It was not as easy as I thought it would be. I remember there were bodyguards and police in the entrance of the theatre and backstage. They did not let me stay around too long. By mid-afternoon, the orchestra had started to set up.

At the backstage door, I recognized a celebrity—Count Basie. I went up to him and introduced myself.

"I am your fan," I told him. He was very kind to me. We spoke of music. "I like to sing, too. I'm here to meet Sammy. Would you be willing to take a photo with me?"

"Sure," he said.

A bystander snapped the shot.

"Do you know when Sammy will be arriving?" I asked Count Basie.

"Around 9 p.m. or so."

"Okay, Mr. Basie. Thank you. Bye."

It was around 6:15 p.m. I went for a quick bite and returned to my post at the stage door at 8 p.m., waiting until around 8:30.

A security guard came up to me. "You can't wait there, sir."

"But I just wanted to take a photo with Sammy," I protested.

"Everyone does," he said.

I moved back just twenty feet. I waited a long time. It was 9:25 p.m. I became a bit worried, not only that I wouldn't see Sammy, but because the last bus was leaving at 11 p.m. So I had to think and do something fast. I moved toward the security guards.

"I'm waiting for Sammy, but I don't see him. Why is that?"

One turned around and said, "Sammy is already here. He's backstage."

"Oh, no!" I said. "I'd like to take a photo with him."

"I'm sorry, sir. He's getting ready to start soon."

"Well, when is the show finished?"

"Around midnight or maybe later. That's usually when the show's over."

I felt so disappointed. I didn't know what to do. Afraid I would never get the chance to see Sammy again, I decided not to take the bus that night. It was crazy, but I was very determined to meet Sammy. I went to a few hotels and found I could not book a room at any of them. I just could not afford it.

It was now around 2 or 3 a.m. Tired, I went to the poolside. There were bleachers there and I lay down on them and rested for a few hours.

At about 5:15 a.m., I looked out over the sea and breathed in the sea air. A new morning began, and the hotel security guard arrived.

"Sir, how long have you been here?"

"For several hours."

"You're not supposed to be here."

"Well, I am just leaving, anyhow."

He made sure I did. He was a very big person.

That was close, I thought. I could have been in trouble for vagrancy. Thank God, I wasn't.

At around 6:45 a.m., I headed for a breakfast diner nearby. It was not too expensive, and I had a great breakfast. I had very little money left. The day was long. The afternoon came, and there I was again, waiting.

The security guard came over and said, "You again!"

"Yes, sir, it's me."

"You don't give up," he replied.

I smiled, "I'm not leaving without a photo with Sammy."

He looked at me. "What makes you think you will have one?"

"'Cause I know I will."

As the evening approached, I found out Sammy was coming by another entrance. I went directly toward that side of the building and lingered. No one else waited yet at the door. I looked at my watch. It was 8:25 p.m. Still no sign of Sammy. Oh no, I thought. I cannot stay another day!

Suddenly, two police officers came. "You can't stay here, sir," one said.

"Look, I've been here since yesterday. The only thing I want is a photo with Sammy." I felt very disappointed again. It was almost 9 p.m.

While they were telling me to leave, I could not believe my eyes. Sammy came toward me with his bodyguards. It is now or never. He turned toward me.

"Sammy, Sammy!" I said loudly. "Can you please take a photo with me?"

Sammy Davis Jr., and me.

He looked at me, stopped and said, "Sure, man. Make it fast."

"Yes, Sammy, thank you, sir."

As we posed for the photo, taken by one of the security guards, we spoke a few words. I told him, "I'm your fan, and I love show business and singing. I want to make it just like you."

He looked at me with a smile. "Keep the faith and determination."

As we said goodbye, I must have thanked him several times. I had finally been near Sammy. After the guards gave me back the camera and I was leaving, I passed the skeptical security guard and smiled. "I told you I would."

I boarded my bus for home at 11 p.m. I wrote to Sammy afterward, mailed my photo to him and thanked him. He replied with a letter and a photo saying, "Hope you continue the career in show business. Keep the faith."

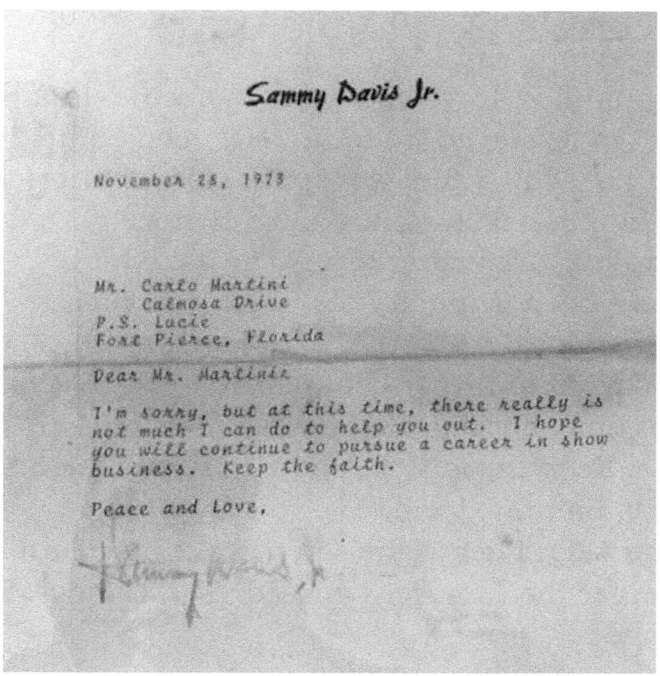

A letter I received from Sammy.

It made me happy to hear from Sammy. I sent the photo to *TV Star Parade Magazine,* and they published it in 1975.

Sammy passed away May 16, 1990.

Today I stay in touch with Sammy Davis' son. His name is Manny Davis. We have developed a friendship.

The last time I saw Sammy Davis, Jr., was in Monte Carlo in 1988. While in Italy, I heard of his show and went to see him at the Hotel de Paris in Monaco. I could not believe my fortune to find him at the bar alone with the barman. I introduced myself once more. "Hi, Sammy, how are you?" I explained the circumstances of having met him in Florida and showed him the photo, letter and magazine article I had carried with me.

He said, "Yeah, man, I recall it a bit. Would you like to join me for a drink?"

"I would love to." I had a glass of wine. He appeared lonely, so I stayed to talk. He seemed to like my company. This time we spoke for about forty-five minutes. I considered it a great honor.

"How long are you in town?" he asked.

"I have been living in Italy for several months," I said. "I took a train to see you."

He smiled and thanked me. As we said goodbye for the last time, he said, "Remember, don't give up on your dreams. Keep the faith in show business, man."

"I will, Sammy. I will."

Years later, I heard the sad news of his death. A great entertainer, he is surely missed. The Candy Man was now gone too.

Ohio

IN 1974, WHILE I RESIDED IN FLORIDA, I DATED SOMEONE FROM Ohio. I had met Janet when she vacationed in Florida with her family. For the few weeks I knew her, we spoke of show business. When she left to return home, she said, "Come visit me. Perhaps you can sing in Ohio."

One month later, I flew to Youngstown where she lived. Her family picked me up at the airport in Pittsburg. I did not know I would stay a month. They made me feel very welcome.

"You should start singing here," my friend said as she showed me the town. She pointed at a venue that looked somewhat like a fairground. "There are many Italian residents here, and you would go over great."

"It sounds good," I said.

"This weekend there's an Italian festival in town, and I'll take you there."

That Sunday afternoon we went to the event—people, music and food. Everyone was dancing and having a great time.

"Come," she said. "I'll introduce you to the people in charge of the show."

I told them in Italian about my singing and my roots in Italy. The director spoke Italian, so we carried on a conversation for a while.

"Would you like to sing here now?" he asked.

"Yes, I'd like that, but I didn't practice with the band."

"Don't worry. They can play anything you like. Just tell them."

The food looked good and smelled so inviting I almost did not want to sing! That afternoon, one of the band members called me to the stage. I sang the theme from *The Godfather* in Italian. I also sang songs from the film *Mondo Cane*, and I did a little Elvis.

When I finished, the audience gave me the warmest applause. It felt like I was in a live concert. Some people came up, shook my hand, congratulated me and invited me to their table to have dinner.

"You see, I was right." Janet sat next to me. "I said you would go over good here!"

She and I had such a great time that we did not even want to go home.

Finally, around 9 p.m. while the fiesta still went on, we pulled ourselves away. As we said goodbye to everyone, the manager of the festival asked, "Where can I reach you?"

"I can give you my number," Janet said. "He's staying at my family's house."

"Okay. You sounded so good, I'd like to schedule you here for a few shows, and I'll pass a good word around about you on to other people."

"Thanks, I appreciate that."

Five days went by. I received a call from ABC-TV in Youngstown, inviting me to appear on the local popular talk program with Margaret Linton, *One Woman's World*. The caller scheduled me for the next week right after the wrestling program. I needed someone to play the piano and had to act fast.

After several calls, I found a great piano player, an African-American man. I told him my story. When I heard him play, it was like magic. We started practicing our show songs and made a great match. We learned "And I Love You So" and other songs from Perry Como's music, as well as some Italian numbers. We wanted to be ready in case they wanted us for more engagements.

Janet went with me to the ABC-TV station. Mrs. Linton, a very nice woman, prepared me to be on the air while my piano player prepared his music. Then, with a little bit of warming up before the show, I went out on the set.

"Carlo will sing for us," Mrs. Linton told her viewers. "Everyone listen to this young man. You will enjoy his voice." I was her guest for the hour that day. I sang "And I Love You So," had an interview with her and then sang another song.

My renditions of "More" and "It's Impossible" impressed her. After the show, she invited me to come back the following week. Excited, my piano player and I practiced new songs the next day. However, I had been in Ohio three weeks, and my savings had dwindled. I wasn't getting paid for these appearances. I had to think fast.

The following week we appeared once more on ABC with Margaret Linton—another great success. Afterward, Janet and I went out to the mall to walk around. People came up to me, saying, "Hey, I heard you sing, and I really liked it. Can I have your autograph?"

"Yeah, sure," I said.

Janet watched me and smiled. As we left, she said, "You're a local celebrity. How do you feel about that?"

"Well, it's nice, but I never imagined people would ask for an autograph. It's great."

"See, if you can stay here, you will make a name for yourself . . . and who knows after that?"

"Yes, it sounds nice, but I'm running out of my savings. I can't stay much longer."

"You must stay because there are still some appearances you need to do."

"But I have only $187 left, and I need to pay for my expenses. I can't live forever at your family's home, though they have been very helpful."

"Actually," she said, "I need to leave with my family for several days."

"Where will I stay?"

"There's a nice family from Italy across the street. You can stay with them for a few days."

After introductions, they took care of me and fed me. I wanted to pay for my room and board. They did not want me to. I thanked them from the bottom of my heart.

For the few days I stayed, I felt welcome. The woman of the house cooked great meals. I knew I would not go hungry there.

I called my mom just about every day for one month. "I'm staying with an Italian family, and they are taking care of me."

"I'm so happy to hear that."

The few days I spent there, they took me to shows and Italian parties. I felt that I was in great company.

My friend returned with her family, and I went back to stay with them for a few more days. Then I went back to Florida.

Pittsburg

BEFORE I LEFT YOUNGSTOWN, I HAD A PHONE CALL FROM A VOICE teacher, a promoter for shows. He saw me on TV and wanted to help my career. He offered to meet me soon and train me for better projects. He lived in the Pittsburg area, a short distance from Youngstown.

"I don't have much money left, and I need to return home soon," I told him.

"Don't worry," he said. "You'll be staying at an apartment we have set up. And below there's a little Italian ristorante."

"Well, it sounds great, but I can't afford it." I said. Nevertheless, I took a chance.

Janet and I drove to see him. A little room in an old brick apartment occupied part of the floor above the downstairs restaurant.

"You make yourself at home," he said.

"Okay, sir!" I took the position, but I had my doubts. I thanked him and returned to Ohio to gather my possessions.

The following day at 6 p.m., my friend and her family dropped me off. We said our goodbyes for the last time. I never saw Janet again.

I settled in Pittsburg—all alone with only $75.55 in my wallet. I canceled my return plane fare, which gave me another $180. Not having much money, it was a huge step on a chance. The man seemed honest.

I subsisted on club sandwiches. They were not the meals I had back in Ohio. The menu at the restaurant was very simple. However, I had to get transportation for every place I needed to go. I walked to the bus station, the only thing close. I lived in the middle of nowhere. Luckily, around the corner, just a few minutes away, a little shop offered donuts and coffee in the mornings.

One day I was talking with the promoter in his office. "The performance you did on that TV show in Ohio—you sounded great! We'll start voice lessons soon. You'll be singing on a big show not far from here in a club. This could launch your career, when we sponsor you."

The promoter told me that he was going to schedule me to sing before Frank Sinatra Jr. He predicted it was going to be my big break.

I was so excited that I called to tell my mom the good news. When my father answered the phone he said, "I need you to come home. Your mom is in the hospital." It was not what I wanted to hear. I was so worried about my mom, and I was also worried about how I would survive financially for a long time. However, that was not what was most important. I loved my mom and she needed me.

I had to go back and tell the promoter that I could not accept the contract now, that my mom had fallen ill and I needed to be with her. Even though the show would not go on for another month, he did understand that my mom needed me more at that time. I thanked him for understanding and said I would be in touch.

Even though I knew I could not stay, I told him I was sorry and that I really had to leave. However, I never heard from him again.

I was still thinking of my way to get home. By this time I only had $95 to my name. I had to pay for my ticket, which cost me $65 one way on a Greyhound bus.

I bought my ticket and left the next morning for Florida with only $30 left. I knew I had to spend it wisely . . . not much money to survive a two-day trip.

I survived with little food. The first day we stopped along the way to relax. As everyone left the bus for a meal, I realized I could not purchase much. I stocked up on ginger ale and a few bags of pretzels, which cost close to five dollars.

The nights seemed endless. I munched away, hoping I would fall asleep.

At 1 a.m., when everyone else slept, there I sat with my eyes open. Perhaps I could just doze off for one hour.

I was still awake at 5:22 a.m. Florida seemed a long distance away.

At 7 a.m., near Kentucky, we stopped at a coffee shop, and I ordered a breakfast. I had to fuel myself for a change. Since we had a one-hour stay, I felt I should eat as much as I could so I would not get hungry. By now I only had $5.75 left in my wallet. I thought, *Only a miracle can take care of me now.*

As we left the coffee shop, I thought, I have to survive. I had no one there to help me out. When we made a stop near Nashville for more passengers, I sat alone by a window.

"Is this seat taken?" a man said to me. He was young but older than I was and tall with curly hair. He gestured at the seat next to me.

"No, it's not."

I wondered, Why the seat next to me? When there are all these other options of seats to sit in? I felt timid, hungry and too worried to be sociable. However, as the bus left, we started to talk. We spoke of music and religion.

"I'm David, by the way." He smiled at me and asked me if I believed in God and in Jesus. "You have to have faith," he said.

I told him about myself and my trip to Ohio. I did not want to tell him I had only five dollars in my wallet and that my pretzels were running out.

"Where you headed, Carlo?"

"Florida."

"Oh, I'm getting off in Atlanta. So we both have a bit of a journey ahead."

"Yes," I sighed. "I've been on board for many hours, and I'd sure like to reach Florida soon."

At about 9 a.m., we arrived near the border between North Carolina and South Carolina. There we stopped for another meal at a rest stop diner. I was very hungry.

"Are you getting anything?" he asked.

"Ah, no, not really. I'm not that hungry."

"You must be hungry. You better eat—you still have a long way to go."

"I know. I thank you for being concerned."

I sat at a table with him. He started eating, then looked at me and said, "I can't believe you're not eating."

Well, I just could not hide it any longer. I told him my situation.

"You're kidding."

"No, I'm not." I showed him I was broke. Well, almost. I only had $5.75.

"Oh, no. Come on, lunch is on me. How's that sound? Good?"

"Oh, no, I don't want to trouble you."

"Oh, Carlo, it's no trouble. Come on—order anything you like."

As I did, I was thinking of miracles and thought of his preaching to me in the bus, about the Lord Jesus. I thought, Jesus caused me to be introduced to this nice young man. I am so grateful he did!

I felt better after a good lunch in the company of this kind person. I felt I had known him for years. Back on our bus, he told me about Elvis.

"Oh, my God! Do you know him?" I asked.

"Well, I can say I spoke with him several times."

"Oh, really? Wow!"

"I know the members of his band."

I happily listened to his story. It made me feel better during the long trip. We fell asleep. The trip for him would soon end.

We awoke. Soon he turned to me and said, "Well, Carlo, this is where I get off." We had reached the Atlanta bus station. "You take care and please be careful."

I did not know how to thank him for what he had done for me. Such a polite and helpful person.

"Thank you so much," I said. "Bye."

He left the bus but then came right back.

"I'd like to give you something," he said. He handed me two, twenty-dollar bills.

"Oh, I can't take this, David."

"Please take it. You still have a long way, and you cannot live on five dollars. You must have a good meal." As he left again, he said, "Always have faith in the Lord!"

"Thank you so very much," I called after him.

After he left, I sat alone, wondering. I thanked Jesus for his blessing of sending David. I reached my destination of West Palm Beach Bus Terminal, and there my father waited. I was so happy to see him and to be so close to home.

I visited my mom, who was soon to be released from the hospital, and told her of this young man who helped me.

"Son," she said, "Jesus is with you, and he sent this person for you."

"Well, I hope I'll see him again."

"If you don't, just pray and have faith like he said you must do. And be thankful for the things God does for us."

To this day, I wonder what happened to my friend on the bus. Nevertheless, wherever he may be, I always remember his words and always have faith in the Lord.

Backstage at the Grand Ole Opry

I FIRST VISITED THE GRAND OLE OPRY IN MAY 1975. I had visited Nashville many times before for the purpose of recording music. Recording *Carlo's Country*, my first CD, brought me there again. This time I stayed near the Opry. I hoped I would be able to do the show on Saturday evening. I had an unsuccessful search for tickets. It had sold out.

After dinner the night of the Opry show, I listened to some music in the downstairs lounge in the hotel where a female singer, Charlotte, performed. She sounded great. I stayed to listen to her. When she had a break, I went up to the stage and introduced myself. I told her of my singing.

"Do you want to sing?" she asked.

"I would love to."

In Nashville, it's very unusual to be invited on stage. I sang a few songs, and as I stepped off the platform, she took her break.

"The Opry is sold out," I told her. "I had so hoped to see it."

"I can make it happen," she said. "Follow me, and I'll introduce you to some people." She walked over to a table in the lounge where two men sat.

"Everyone, I would like to introduce Carlo Martini," she said. They invited me to sit with them. I told them about my career and about my dream to see the Opry. "I don't have tickets to see the show tonight. I can't get in."

"I tell you what," one of the men said. "We are going around 9:00 this evening. Would you like to go with us?"

"Yes! But it's sold out."

"Don't worry." He said, "We can go backstage with no problem."

"Are you serious?"

"Yes. Just meet us here at 8:45 p.m."

"Thank you!" I rejoined them promptly at 8:45 p.m. We parked near security and walked a few minutes to the entrance. It seemed everyone knew the man who had invited me. *Who is he? I wondered.* I did not want to ask. We all went in through the back doors. I could not believe I entered backstage at the Opry and did not even have tickets.

We walked down the corridor. My host turned to me and said, "Carlo, you are in the dressing room area of the stars."

"What if they ask me about a pass? I don't have one."

"That's okay. You're with me, but if there is a problem, just tell them I'm sitting there in the front row."

"Thank you for giving me this opportunity."

"Well, I'm off to see the show. You can stay backstage. You'll be fine."

"Okay, bye." As he left, I mingled with the people and soon saw many of my best-loved country stars. There was Hank Snow!

I introduced myself as I passed by his dressing room where he was preparing for the show.

"Hi, Mr. Snow."

THE GRAND OLE OPRY

"Hi," he said with a smile.

"It is a great pleasure to meet you." He did not have much time to speak with me, but he seemed very cordial.

As I continued on, I saw Jimmy Dickens.

"Hi, Mr. Dickens, remember me?" I said happily, hoping he would remember me.

"Oh, yes. You're the boy that sang in Florida for me."

"Yes, I am. Thank you for having me." I was so flattered that he remembered me. That always makes you feel good.

"Well, are you singing here this evening?"

"No, Jimmy, I'm not. I wish."

"Maybe one day. Just keep dreaming, and maybe we'll see you here. Take care."

"You take care. Bye, Jimmy."

As I turned around, right next to me stood a man. "Hello," he said.

"Hi," I replied. I could not see him well because of the dim lights. The show must have just started. After talking a few minutes, I recognized him—Marty Robbins. One of my favorite singers! We spoke about music, my singing and even about racing. I told him of my admiration for him. He said, "If you have a dream, keep on, and don't let anyone destroy your dreams. Don't give up. Be persistent."

"Okay, Mr. Robbins. I will."

"Would you like to sing at the Opry?" he asked.

"Oh really, Mr. Robbins? That would be great!"

"Well, I will see what I can do."

"You mean that?"

"I will try. I didn't promise, okay?"

Mr. Robbins asked me about my latest 45 single, "I Can See Forever in Your Eyes," and I felt a rush come over me. My heart pounded at a hundred miles a minute.

"I happen to have my record here," I said. I gave him the single and some photos.

"Good," he said. "I will see what I can do. I will have my agent call you."

"Thanks, Mr. Robbins." He seemed to be such a down-to-earth man.

After we finished talking, I spotted a chair backstage and watched the show until it ended around 11 p.m. When the final curtain came down, I stayed until the last person left.

"The Opry is closing," a security guard said.

"Will it be okay if I walk out on the stage?" I asked. The guard nodded.

It felt amazing to walk toward the stage. *I am on the same stage that the country stars sing on.* I am right on the X mark. I found the mic still on and felt I must sing. I heard my voice up there . . . beautiful . . . dreaming again . . . I was singing a few bars when I heard a voice.

"Hey, you sounded good." It was a lady standing up in the balcony.

The security guard finally returned. "Time to leave," he told me.

I looked up at the balcony but saw the lady was no longer there.

As I walked out, I turned back to see the beautiful stage and dreamed once more of singing there.

I never got the chance to appear at the Opry yet, but I know I will one day. I believe in my dreams and I have faith. Some dreams do not come true, but I know mine will.

However, that day on that stage . . . that moment at the Grand Ole Opry . . . it was surreal. I know I will go back and this time they will be calling my name to come out and sing. "Now welcome Mr. Carlo Martini!" Everyone will give me the greatest applause I have ever had.

A Gift for Elvis

In February 1977, I heard Elvis was coming to West Palm Beach Auditorium and staying at the Sheraton. I tried my best to get tickets, but the concert sold out. Knowing his next concert in the area would be too far in the future, I decided to try to get in without tickets with a friend of mine, Reed Walker Jr., who always reminded me of a young Dick Van Dyke. We decided to rent a limo.

"Where shall we pick you up?" the man who answered the phone asked.

"Walgreens store. Inside the mall."

"What?" He thought it was a joke. They didn't get a lot of calls from Walgreens.

Before long, we headed toward the Sheraton with David, the limo driver and a plaque gift specially made for Elvis. It had an engraved religious cross. It said:

TO ELVIS:
OUR LASTING FRIENDSHIP
CARLO MARTINI

As we went toward West Palm Beach, I sensed the excitement of the moment. Once more in my life, I was on my way to see Elvis.

A Gift for Elvis

The limo I rode in to see Elvis in February of 1977.
Walgreens is in the background.

It was 3:15 p.m. when we pulled up at the Sheraton. His appearance would be at about 9 p.m. We tried with great difficulty to find a parking space. Every spot was taken. We decided to drive around to the back by the pool.

There we saw a bunch of people waiting to see Elvis. The parking was impossible. As we looked for a space to park in, the people saw our limo and thought Elvis had arrived. All of a sudden, a mob of people descended on us. What a feeling . . . a glimpse of what widespread fame is really like. I thought to myself, *Now I know what Elvis feels like!* They came toward us, taking photos, following the limo. At this point, a police car arrived. The police officer saw the crowd and apparently thought Elvis rode inside the limo.

Reed laughed. "I can't believe what's happening."

Neither could I. I did not plan it to be like this.

The police officer escorted us to the entrance door of the hotel. As I stepped out, I had long sideburns and hair like Elvis, and some people actually screamed, but they quickly saw I was not him. In unison, they went, "Oh, no." I am sure it disappointed them, but I had not tried to spoil their dream.

I went in and asked where I could take the gift for Elvis. Several people stood at the front entrance. I went directly to the front desk to ask for Elvis' manager, but they didn't want to give me the room numbers. I turned around, and there in the lobby I saw the comedian who opened every show for him. I asked him where I could find Elvis to present my gift to him.

"It's impossible, son," he said. "What can I do?"

"What about Joe Esposito, his manager?"

"Well, they're getting ready, and everyone is in their rooms. I am sorry. I can't help you, son."

"Okay, sir, thank you."

I had to think of something as I waited there. I made my decision. I had seen several people who worked with Elvis going upstairs, and I asked them if I could accompany them. No luck. The security was very strong in every hall and on every floor. What am I going to do now?

It was around 7:15 p.m., and soon the show would start. I had to try something quickly. My best idea: pick up the phone and call a room.

I dialed the first thing that came to my mind and by chance reached Sam, one of Elvis' bodyguards. I introduced myself on the phone and explained my story and the gift. I even told him about Germany. He listened.

"Where are you?" he asked.

"I'm on the main floor in the lobby."

"What type of gift do you have for Elvis?"

"I have a plaque with a cross on it with his name and my name. I am sure Elvis will like this very much. Can I see him?"

"It's very difficult, Carlo," he said. "But I tell you what. I'll talk to Joe and tell him you're downstairs."

"Really? You will do this for me?"

"Yes, but I can't promise they'll have time to come down and pick up the gift."

"But I want Elvis to have it."

"Okay, you stay there."

I thanked him and said goodbye. I stayed near the elevators. I felt a bit worried that this gift would never be given to Elvis personally. I waited there for a while. Suddenly the elevator doors opened up, and there was Joe and a bodyguard.

"Are you Carlo?" Joe said.

"Yes, I am."

"I hear you have a gift for Elvis."

"Yes I do." I opened it to show it to him.

"That's very nice of you." He took the gift, lifted the plaque carefully from the box, looked at it and placed it gently back in. "I know Elvis will like your sentiment."

As I said goodbye at the elevators, I rejoiced that they would give my gift to Elvis, even though I felt sad that I did not get to give it to him personally. It disappointed me that I could not see him. I wanted to stay longer and perhaps see him when he came out of the building for the show, and I started having doubts that he would receive the gift at all. I marched toward the phone and dialed the extension of his bodyguard again.

"Hello, this is Carlo. I'm sorry to bother you, but I am concerned whether my gift was handed to Elvis."

"Yes, it was, and Elvis is looking at it right now. He is having dinner, chicken with gravy tonight, and he is very happy that you gave him this gift. He is thanking you and sending you a blessing."

"Wow," I said. "Elvis is thanking me, and he is happy? Send my hellos."

"I will, Carlo, I will."

"By the way, tell him of Germany, okay?"

83

"I will. Bye. We have to get ready. Bye."

"Thank you again."

The time of the show neared, and everyone was getting ready. Several more fans remained to see if they could get a glimpse of Elvis. No one knew where he would come out. I heard in the hall: "Yeah, he's coming this way," and "No, he's coming from the side doors."

I considered the backdoor steps . . . I went for it with my friend Reed.

Well, bingo, that is where he came out. As I opened the door to the back steps, the police were already there. Oh no, what am I going to do now?

The security guard said, "You can't stay here, sir. You have to go on out the door." While he was saying that, you could hear voices coming from upstairs. They were getting closer. As I started to go, I looked back. Elvis was twenty feet behind me. However, I had to leave to make way for him. I had no choice.

I opened the door. WAMO! All kinds of fans pressed in, waiting for Elvis. I immediately turned to look, and at that moment, Elvis passed me. I snapped a photo as his bodyguard rushed him into the limo. People were everywhere. I could not believe it. I had been near Elvis one more time.

The picture was taken in Florida by photographer Keith Alverson, used by permission. I am to the left of the door.

A Gift for Elvis

In this photo, as he left the Sheraton, Elvis is carrying the plaque gift I gave him. Used by permission.

As they began to drive away from the concert, I went to his window to say hello.

He looked at me, and Joe whispered something to him. He looked through the back window of the limo and gave me a smile and a wave. I knew then he really appreciated my gift. That was the last time I saw Elvis.

As the months went by, I periodically wrote letters to Graceland and hoped Elvis would respond to me. I continued to sing, and in my act, I always included a special tribute to the King.

I was in Florida preparing for a show when I heard the terrible announcement on the radio. I could not believe it. That afternoon held shock for everyone. Elvis was gone.

I was in tears. I thought at first it might be a mistake, but it was not. Elvis was gone.

That evening I found the show to be the most difficult one I ever performed. I could not be at my best. I devoted my entire program to Elvis and his memory.

Near the end, when the lights went down, the fans in the audience lit candles and lighters for several minutes in loving remembrance of Elvis.

Graceland

IN 1978, I VISITED MEMPHIS AND WENT TO GRACELAND. Looking at the house without Elvis made it a painful day for me.

Everything seemed so quiet that morning. Several people wrote their names on the wall that surrounds the property, and I felt the need to do the same.

As I walked across the street to the coffee shop, I felt so empty inside. It was like losing someone in my family. I still could not believe Elvis was gone. I did not want to believe it.

Fans came from everywhere to see Graceland. At one point, I talked to some of them. They told me their stories and their feelings about Elvis. As I told mine, a woman approached me and introduced herself.

"My name is Mrs. Adel," she said. "I heard you speaking of Elvis. I find your story very interesting."

"Thank you, Mrs. Adel."

We continued to converse. I told her after visiting Graceland and Memphis, I would be leaving in four days to return to Florida.

"How would you like to drive through the gates at Graceland tonight?" she asked me.

"What? Are you kidding? I can't do that."

"Well, I can, and you're invited. I know Elvis' cousin, Harold Loyd. He's my friend."

"Oh, wow! That's a dream come true, Mrs. Adel." For a moment, I still thought she might be making a joke.

Then she said, "Look, I will prove it."

She sounded honest, so I took the chance. "Okay, where do I meet you?"

"I'll pick you up, and we'll go there." I had told her I was staying in a hotel very close to Graceland.

"Okay, what time?"

"I will meet you just right after midnight."

"Sure, I'll be there."

I hope she is serious, I thought.

Well, I went back at midnight, and there she was indeed. I got in her car, and we drove to Graceland.

She made a left turn into the entrance of the estate, and the gates opened up. *Oh, my goodness,* I thought to myself. I cannot believe it. She is driving me inside the gates. A security man stood by the guardhouse as we parked. We walked up to the guardhouse, and Mrs. Adel introduced me to Harold Loyd.

"Carlo, this is Elvis' cousin."

"Hello," I said. "Nice to meet you, sir."

I told him some of my stories. He looked at me with interest, and I could tell we were going to be good friends.

Harold Loyd and me at the Graceland gates.

"Come on with me and have a seat in the guardhouse," he said.

I was sitting in the guardhouse with Harold and Mrs. Adel. A few minutes later, another friend of Elvis' came in. We talked until about 3:25 in the morning.

"It's too bad that Elvis didn't get to know you," Harold said. "He would have really liked you. You have a lot in common with him."

"I would have loved that."

"He would have liked you as a friend," he went on. I had difficulty believing what he said.

Harold told me to come over the following night. He would be at the guardhouse, and we could talk some more.

"Thank you for the invitation," I said. "I will be here."

As we left the gates, I felt like I was in a dream, but I convinced myself it was really happening. I just wish it could have happened when Elvis was alive.

Mrs. Adel had loaned me her car, so the following day I visited some places that had been important to Elvis. I went to the high school Elvis had attended. I also went by his apartment. As I drove by, for a minute I felt like I was back in the time when he had lived there. I looked at the apartment and hoped to see Elvis coming out. Still dreaming . . . I knew that would not bring him back. He was gone.

I decided to see some other sites. When I arrived at Sun Records Studio, I imagined Elvis pulling up in his little pickup truck. I parked next to the studio where he went to record for the first time.

I went to the little diner next to Sun Records Studio where Elvis used to go. It's still there today. It was lunchtime.

When I went in, I felt once more like I had stepped back in time. Everything looked like it did back when Elvis lived. Only a few people sat at the tables.

"Can I help you?" a server asked.

"Yes. I would like a hamburger, fries and a small Coke."

"Okay."

As I waited for my order, I chose a table near the windows. Not realizing it, I had picked the same booth Elvis sat in to sign his first contract.

I looked out the window and saw a man wearing a beret who appeared to be in his forties. He came in the diner and walked up to my table with a Coke in his hand. I guess he saw I wore my hair like Elvis did.

"My name is Gene," he said. "I live in Memphis. I knew Elvis in high school. We were really good friends, Elvis and I. He used to call me Weenie Burger."

Me in 2012 with Gene Mason (12/22/35–4/6/15). He had become my good friend since 1978. Photo used by permission of his family in his memory. He was inducted in the Memphis Rock and Roll Hall of Fame.

"Oh? I wish I had been there to know him. Would you care to join me?" My hamburger had arrived.

He sat down and placed his Coke on the table. "Did you know Elvis sat here, looked out that same window and ordered from the same menu?"

My girlfriend, Debra, and me in 2010, sitting at the same booth I sat at in 1978.

"Really? Are you kidding me?"

"No," he replied.

The server came over to bring me my bill, and Gene introduced me to her. He said she had been the one who waited on Elvis. This week she was retiring from the diner. She told me she served Elvis the same thing she served me. Then she said I reminded her of Elvis. I loved hearing these compliments. I felt honored. I gave her a hug and thanked her for being my server too.

"Are you coming back here?" Gene asked.

"I don't know. I'm leaving in a few days."

"Well, here's my phone number. Give me a call sometime."

"Okay, Gene, I will."

"Lunch is on me," Gene said.

"Thank you." Little did I know, this was the beginning of a lasting friendship.

The evening approached. Although tired, I had a promise to keep with Harold Loyd. I called Mrs. Adel to let her know I would be at the gates around 12:15 a.m.

I rested for a while in my hotel room and must have fallen asleep because when I woke up it was 1:05 a.m. I immediately got up and called Harold at the guardhouse.

"Carlo, where are you? Are you coming?"

"Yes, I am, Harold. I am sorry. I fell asleep."

"Okay. We're waiting for you."

I got dressed and flew out the door like Superman. In ten minutes, I arrived at the gates. They opened immediately for me. I pulled in next to the guardhouse.

"Come on in," Harold said. "Several people are here."

Another one of Elvis' cousins was there, and Mrs. Adel was there too. We had a great evening keeping Harold company. Harold took a photo for me of me driving through the gates of Graceland.

Ms. Adel and me inside the Graceland gates.
Harold took the picture for us.

It was the early hours of the morning. The gates opened suddenly and a man drove in. Harold spoke to him for a few minutes and then turned to me. "Carlo, I want to introduce you to Elvis' dad," he said.

Oh, my goodness, I thought. I cannot believe it.

"Vernon, this is Carlo."

"Hi, how are you, son?" he said.

"Fine, sir."

He smiled at me as I told him how much I cared for Elvis and what a big fan I was.

"Thank you," he said. "Everybody loved him."

Vernon seemed in a hurry, so I did not want to take up much of his time.

"It was such an honor to meet you, Mr. Presley," I said.

He looked at me as he shook my hand. "Son, the pleasure is all mine." *I spoke with Elvis' daddy,* I thought. That nice man unfortunately passed away a few years later.

When I left that morning, I marked this as a great moment in my life.

"You come over and visit Graceland anytime," Harold told me before I left. "Okay?"

"Thank you, Harold. I will."

Uncle Vaster, Vernon's brother, and me on Elvis' golf cart in 1978.

Elvis' Circle G Ranch

In the early '80s, there was a great moment in my life. I had a job at Elvis' Ranch in Walls, Mississippi, near Graceland.

Gene Mason introduced me to the owner, a man named Buddy Montesi. Buddy liked me right away. We went back to the ranch a few days later, and Buddy asked if I would be interested in working there along with Harold Loyd and many others of Elvis' family.

"We are going to be opening soon and offering tours for the fans, and we could let you sing here sometimes."

He invited me upstairs to his office to discuss the employment. Mr. Montesi had all kinds of personal souvenirs from Elvis such as guitars, shoes and shirts.

"You will be responsible for putting everything in its place, like a museum. It will be your job to take care of the property. It needs a bit of work here and there."

"I would love that," I said.

"You can stay in the little cottage Elvis and Priscilla used as a get-a-way."

He told me a story about how Elvis had lost his wedding ring. He had been riding his horse when he lost it. I was so amazed at the stories.

"Are you interested in the job?" he asked.

"I am very interested."

"I'll call you when it is time for you to start."

I was so excited on the ride back to Gene's house! It was as if Elvis had chosen me. I would soon be working on his ranch. When I got home, I told my mom all about the things I had experienced on that trip and the things planned. She was very happy for me.

Weeks later, I received a letter from Memphis, telling me that the ranch sold to new owners. My dream did not turn out as I had wished.

I still had my memories to cherish for the rest of my life. I always recall with great fondness my trips to Memphis and my visits to Graceland. Even though Elvis is no longer here, he will always live in my heart.

Aunt Lorraine and Others in Elvis' Family

In 1978, while in Memphis, I became friends with Elvis' aunt—Aunt Lorraine Smith. Aunt Lorraine was the sister of Gladys, Elvis' mother. I had the pleasure of meeting her in Memphis when I sang at a club. Gene and Mrs. Adel had arranged a couple of gigs for me. Mrs. Smith came to the show and someone introduced us. I even danced with her.

"I like the way you sing," she said. "Particularly the way you sing the Elvis songs."

"Thank you very much. It is an honor to sing Elvis' music and to pay tribute to him."

"When are you returning to Memphis?"

"I will be back soon," I told her.

"You call me sometime, okay?" she said.

"Okay."

She adopted me, so to speak, and told me to call her "Aunt Lorraine." We said our goodbyes that evening, and I now had another friend. *Oh, I wish Elvis were here*, I thought.

I kept my promise to Aunt Lorraine. I phoned her several times and always when I was in Memphis.

She invited me to her apartment once, located behind the souvenir shops, across the road and up a hill from Graceland.

Aunt Lorraine Smith and me.

She showed me a beautiful piece of Indian jewelry with a cross on it. "Elvis gave me this necklace," she told me. "He came over late so no one would know. Elvis has been in this very same apartment."

"Wow!" I said. "He gave you a great gift."

"Would you like to try it on?"

"Oh, Aunt Lorraine, I could not do that."

"Please, try it on."

As I tried it on, it gave me a wild feeling knowing that Elvis had given her the necklace.

"Elvis is a wonderful person," I said. "I gave him a plaque, and it is now in the Trophy Room at Graceland. I saw it on my first visit after the Trophy Room opened."

"I'm sure he loved it," she said. Standing on her doorstep, she waved goodbye to me. It was the last time I saw Aunt Lorraine. She passed away several years later—a wonderful woman and a great friend, I will remember her always.

. . .

The years went by, and starting in the '80s when I was living in New Jersey, I made sure every year I went to Graceland to pay my respects.

Through the years, I made friends with the rest of Elvis' family. I met Priscilla Presley, Billy Smith, Jesse Pritchett and Uncle Vester.

I also met some of Elvis' friends such as Joe Esposito, Charlie Hodge and J.D. Summer and the Stamps Quartet. In 1989, I performed in the same show as J.D. Summer and sang two gospel songs before he came on.

Me with Jimmy Velvet, a good friend of Elvis, in New Jersey.

Me with The Drifters when we all appeared at the Asbury Park Convention Hall in New Jersey.

Me with Danny Aiello in 1982 at Asbury Park Convention Hall.

Ginger Alden

A FEW WEEKS AFTER THE DEATH OF MY IDOL, ELVIS PRESLEY, the greatest entertainer in the world, I decided to look for the phone number of Ginger Alden to offer her my condolences. Ginger had been his fiancée.

I called Information. The operator found the number easily because I had the address. The listing was her mom and dad's number. She did not live with them anymore, but I took the chance that she would be there.

I dialed the number.

"Hello, may I speak with Ginger, please?" I felt very excited. "Do I have the right number?"

A young voice answered. "Yes, you do. Who is this?"

"I'm Carlo. Who am I speaking with?"

"This is Terri, Ginger's sister."

"Oh, hi, Terri. I'm calling to see if I could speak with Ginger, please."

"Well, she's not here at the moment."

"When can I call her back?"

"She will be in later."

"Okay. Please tell her I called."

Later in the evening, I called back. I spoke with Ginger this time.

"I am very sorry to hear about Elvis," I said.

"It was a shock for everyone," she replied. "I loved him very much." We talked for a couple minutes. As we concluded the conversation, she said, "Thank you for calling."

"I will write you a letter real soon," I promised.

The next day I wrote her a letter and sent it with a cassette and photo of me. Ginger wrote me back thanking me for the letter and for thinking of her. She told me it helped her a great deal.

Since then I have received from her Christmas cards, letters of congratulations on my career and a signed photo of herself.

I thanked Ginger for her time and for remembering me.

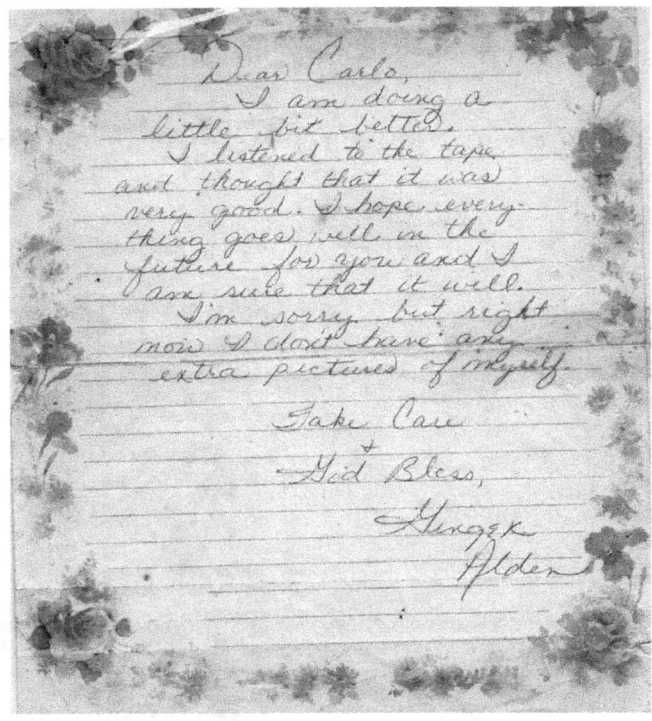

One of the letters that Ginger wrote to me.

Jerry Lewis

I HAD THE PLEASURE OF OPENING FOR SOME CELEBRITIES IN THE LATE '70s at The Diplomat on Collins Avenue in Miami Beach. On separate occasions, I went on before comedienne Elaine Boosler and actor Telly Savalas from Kojak.

I worked as a waiter for a while at the Hilton Hotel in Port St. Lucie, Florida. There were some dinner roasts of celebrities where I went on before performances of Rat Pack member Joey Bishop. Bobbie Riggs was among the guests at one of the roasts. In Florida in 1978, I also appeared on the same show with Gary Lewis, the son of Jerry Lewis.

Joey Bishop and me in Port St. Lucie, Florida.

During that time, Jerry Lewis stayed as a guest at the Port St. Lucie Hilton, singing occasionally on weekends and playing golf. I had watched his films as a child in Italy. *Jerry is in the same place I am,* I thought to myself.

Bobbie Riggs and me in Port St. Lucie, Florida.

One day, Mr. Lewis entered the restaurant with another man. I was serving a different table at the time, so I tried in every way to see if I could be his waiter. I tried appealing to the waiter who was serving him.

"That's my table," he told me.

I explained my situation. "Please just let me bring him the salad."

He looked at me for a moment. "Okay, just the salad."

"Okay, yes, just the salad."

As I went toward the table, my heart rate registered a mile a minute. I could not believe my eyes. I had always wanted to meet Jerry Lewis, and now I was serving him his salad.

"Hi, Jerry," I said. "How are you?"

"Hello," he responded.

"Here is your salad, Jerry." As I put it on the table, I just could not stop myself. I started to tell him how much I liked him and that I had seen his films.

"Thank you," he said. He tried to eat as he listened to me, but every time he tried to eat his salad I came up with another thing to tell him. Finally, I left his table.

"Thanks Jerry, I'll see you later."

I saw the restaurant manager looking at me. As I looked at him, I suddenly understood the expression about smoke coming out of someone's head. He walked toward me.

"Mr. Martini, you were only supposed to serve his salad. That is all!"

"Yes, sir, I know, but I just couldn't help it. I have had a dream to meet him since I was little." He took me aside and continued.

"Well, meet him somewhere else. Not on my time."

WOW, was he upset! He took me away from the tables and put me in the kitchen. But it was far from over. I had to see Jerry one more time.

I had the next day off, so I took a chance and returned to see if I could get another glimpse. I searched but found him nowhere. Then after a few hours, I noticed a golf cart by the shoe shop with Jerry in it and the same fellow who had accompanied him at the restaurant, possibly his photographer. I immediately went toward the golf cart and called his name.

"Jerry, Jerry!" When he saw me, he went into the shop.

Great, I thought. Now I can really have some time like the manager told me.

I went into the store but did not see Jerry. I spoke to a girl who worked behind the counter. "I saw Jerry coming in here," I said, "and I need to talk to him."

"He's not here," she replied.

"I'm sure I saw him come in this store."

"He's not here," she repeated kindly.

I finally left the store, thinking, This will possibly be my only chance to talk to him. I went around the corner to wait. I looked to see if he would come out, and about ten minutes later, there he was. As he came out of the store, he looked around and started to walk toward the Port St. Lucie Hilton marina. I stepped forward. "Jerry, Jerry!"

He saw me and ran. Remembering that this may be my last chance to talk to him, I found myself running after him. Now that I think back, it was just like a comedy film. I finally lost him and went home disappointed. However, I thought, *Tomorrow is another day.*

My mom loved Jerry, so she came with me the next day. This time I saw him coming with his secretary. He was wearing a red jacket with black pants and looked great.

"Hi, Jerry, remember me?" I said. "This is my mother. She wanted to say hello."

As he shook her hand, he said to me, "I saw you yesterday. Weren't you my waiter?"

"Yeah."

"Weren't you also at the shop?"

"Yeah."

"I saw you yesterday plenty of times. I don't have time for you now."

I was surprised at what he said and didn't say anything for a moment. "I always try to donate money and my talent to the muscular dystrophy cause." Jerry Lewis hosted the Muscular Dystrophy Association Labor Day Telethon.

"Thank you," he said and left.

"Thanks, bye." Somehow I knew we would see each other again.

The Mike Douglas Show

A YEAR PASSED. I HEARD THE MIKE DOUGLAS SHOW WAS BEING filmed in 1976 at Miami Beach with Jerry Lewis scheduled for appearances the whole week. I wanted to try to get on the show, so I went to Miami, made a reservation at a hotel nearby and stayed a few days.

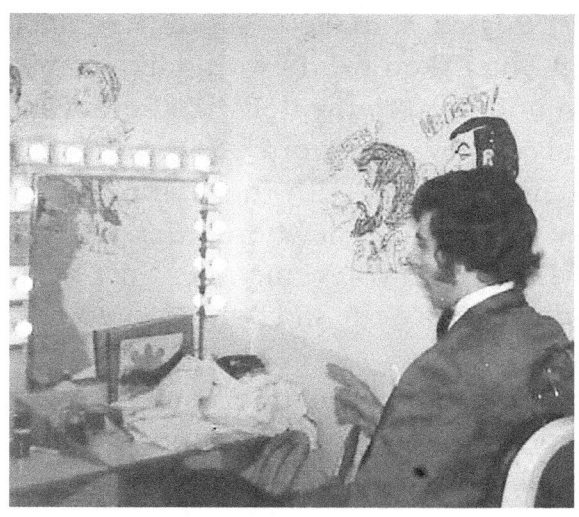

Philadelphia in 1971 while auditioning
for the Mike Douglas show during my high school years.
Photo taken in Mike Douglas show Green Room.

The producers of the Miami Beach show planned to tape it on the shore of the beach, not far from my hotel.

105

The day was beautiful with plenty of sunshine. When I got to the beach, many people sat in the bleachers, waiting for the activities to start. During the show, stars stayed in a tent in the back. I tried to enter the tent without success. The security officers did their job.

Outside the tent, I saw the wrestler André the Giant, a man over seven feet tall. I had seen him before in one of his wrestling matches. He was going to wrestle Mike Douglas and Jerry Lewis as a tag team. I felt the need to approach him and say hello.

I was so small compared to him. I gave him one of my records and told him I wanted to be on the show and see Jerry and the other stars. André told me he couldn't put me on the show, but if I stayed close to him, he could get me in the tent.

Once inside the tent, I saw Carol Lawrence, Mel Tillis and Mike Douglas. I spoke to all of them. Carol was so wonderful! She asked me if I would like some coffee and donuts. In addition, to my delight, there was Jerry!

"Hi, Jerry, how are you?" Everyone who saw us talking knew I came in with the Giant.

"I know you from somewhere," Jerry replied.

"Well," I said, "do you remember Port St. Lucie?"

"Yes I do. You are the kid who wanted to speak with me. The waiter."

Wow, Jerry remembered me! It made me so happy!

"I am such a big fan of yours and love all your films, including those with Dean Martin."

He said, "Come back, and I will see you later."

I was speechless. Jerry told me to wait! I did. I wondered, What does he want to say to me? I waited and waited. The show was about to end and everyone was leaving. I left with the TV crew. Jerry and Mike Douglas were still on the air. I knew when they finished they would come my way. While I waited, a man came up to me and told me I had to leave.

"I'm waiting on Jerry."

"I'm sorry," he said. "Mr. Lewis said you have to leave."

I was so upset. I had come all this way and had waited for Jerry because he told me to, and now I would have to go without speaking with him. Then he told me they took Jerry out the other way where his limo waited. I had no choice but to depart quietly. As I left, I wanted just one more chance to see Jerry. I worked my way until I stood near the limo . . . and then there it went and with it, my last opportunity to see Jerry Lewis.

Frank Sinatra

IN THE SUMMER OF 1978, IN FLORIDA ON A HOT DAY, OL' BLUE Eyes was going to be in Fort Lauderdale at Sunrise Theatre of the Performing Arts. I heard of his arrival. I wanted to see Frank Sinatra. I decided to present him with a plaque.

When I arrived in my Ford Galaxy, I wasted no time. I had already started to think how I might get to Sinatra and knew it would not be easy. Getting through security at the back entrance would be the first challenge. I arrived at the theater and saw a guard standing by the back door.

The security officer said, "What can we do for you?"

I asked for Sinatra's secretary. "I'd like to speak with her."

"Sorry, she can't come to see you."

"Okay, thanks." I left.

Everyone was getting ready for the show at 4:15 p.m. The theater opened so the orchestra could set up. This gave me a chance to see the stage. I thought, *Why not go for it?* I saw a musician coming down the sidewalk carrying drums.

"Do you need help?" I said.

"Oh, yes," he said. "Thanks." I started carrying his instruments toward the stage.

There I stood on stage . . . a few musicians and I . . . no audience. It was my chance to see how it felt to be standing in the middle of the same stage where Sinatra would soon be singing. What a feeling! It felt like a dreamland. Fortunately, the mic was on. I started singing a beautiful Italian song, "O Sole Mio." In English, "Oh, my sun."

"Hey, you sing well," someone said. It was the drummer.

"Thank you," I said. While I spoke with him, I heard a security guard calling me.

"Yes?" I said with a smile.

"What are you doing on stage? Who are you? Are you with the show this evening?"

"Well, ah . . . no. I am a singer. I am just trying to get the feel of it on the same stage as Sinatra."

"Well, sir, you have to come down."

"Yes, sir, I will. I am sorry. I didn't mean to cause any trouble."

"What's in the box?"

"Oh," I said. "That is a gift for Frank Sinatra."

"What is it?"

I opened the box and showed him the gift inside.

"Okay, I'll be glad to bring it to him," the guard said.

"I appreciate that, but I'd like to bring it myself."

"It's impossible, sir."

"Can I speak with his secretary?"

"No, she is busy."

"Well, then I'll wait here."

Things were getting a bit hot, but I stood firm. My determination made them go and get her. After a few minutes, here she came. As I introduced myself and explained to her the reason I was there, she smiled. "Please follow me," she said.

We went toward the backstage dressing rooms, but when she reached the hall, she stopped.

"Thank you so much for your lovely gift," she said. "I'll make sure he gets it."

"Is there any way I can see him?"

"He's very busy and doesn't come out until a few minutes before the show starts." She paused, waiting for me to leave. "That's the best I can do," she said firmly. "I'll make sure he gets it."

"Thank you. Okay, bye."

However, that did not stop me. I set out to leave the building, but I went directly to where he would be arriving. It was early afternoon. He would be in the limo, escorted by police on motorcycles like the president of the United States.

As the limo arrived, I was standing right where it pulled up. I tried to ask for a photo but the guards were very intent on taking him into the theater. He passed right next to me while they escorted him in. I would not give up my dream of a photo with Sinatra, so I decided to follow the escort and made it in through the doors. What a lucky moment!

As they took him into the dressing room, I was still determined to see if I could take a photo. I was a bit scared, not knowing what would happen. I went for it.

There he was, several feet away . . . Mr. Sinatra, getting ready for his show. I really did not know what to do.

Frozen like a popsicle, I was afraid to approach him and didn't want to get in any more trouble.

Just as I mustered the courage to ask him for a photo, two big fellows grabbed me by each arm, yelling simultaneously, "What do you think you're doing?! What are you doing here?"

"I'd like to take a photo with Sinatra."

"Everyone has the same request, sir."

I tried to explain my reason, but they seemed not to care. They let go of my arms and escorted me out. As I walked with them toward the door, I noticed several people in line, and I guess they saw me with this entourage escorting me. Maybe they thought I was someone famous. They started taking pictures and asked for my autograph. I thought, What a great feeling! Why spoil a good thing?

I stopped and started signing and posing for photos. Those big boys seemed a bit surprised. One said to me, "Who are you?"

"Don't you know? I am a singer, Carlo Martini. You'll remember me one day."

They looked at each other with surprise and gave me a big smile. Now they escorted me in a dignified manner. People still asked for my autograph as I said goodbye to them. I went back to my old Galaxy that waited patiently for my return home. It was a very memorable experience in my life.

Future Stars on the Coast of Florida

IN THE LATE '70S, WHILE I WAS LIVING AT PORT ST. LUCIE ON THE east coast of Florida, I performed whenever I could. I had developed friendships with a circle of entertainers at that time. I did not know that some would become well-known celebrities.

I went to Miami frequently to sing in various talent shows. They were held every Wednesday and Saturday nights downstairs at The Diplomat on Collins Avenue in Miami Beach.

I sometimes sat with identical twins who were little people. They were the Rice Brothers, John and Greg. Realtors when not performing, they went on to star in TV spots, including commercials and numerous episodes of the sitcom *Foul Play*. John died in 2005.

Heather Locklear was a young woman I met in those years. We walked together on the beach at times. She went to the West Coast one day, and I never heard from her again. She became a very big star!

Donna Rice was an actress and model I also knew from those days in Miami Beach. She appeared on several TV shows and commercials.

When I sang in the Holiday Inn in nearby Fort Pierce, I recall a band playing there—"The Miami Sound Machine." Today their fame reaches all over the world, led by a wonderful singer. She was a powerful, small woman who had a fascinating voice and an original style. Her name was Gloria Estefan.

Today Gloria is a celebrity. I remember I used to go see her when I did not have a singing engagement. She invited me several times to her shows, not only in the Fort Pierce Holiday Inn, but also in Miami. Her husband played in the band. I always wanted to sing with their band, but they didn't accept my offer. However, Gloria asked me if I wanted to join the band to play bass. I was not good enough on the instrument so I could not accept. I also became friends with Bob Anderson, an impressionist. We are still friends today.

One evening while I was singing Elvis at the Holiday Inn in Fort Pierce, I recall I spoke with a man who passed through the community with a member of his family. We became "passing through friends." This was in the late '70s. He looked out for me much like a bodyguard.

The next day he showed me a martial art called *aikido*. I was fascinated by his magic moves.

I could not help but ask questions. He always responded, taking time to teach me. He spoke of his time living in Japan. It was fascinating to me to hear of the customs there.

"In life, never give up," he frequently said. "Be persistent, meditate and believe in yourself."

We did some hand movements designed to test speed, focus and reflexes. He placed his extended hands palms up, and I, while facing him, placed my palms up beneath his hands. The goal is for the person on the bottom to flip his hands up and touch the palms of the person on top before the top person can remove his hands. In performing this activity with me, he taught me to be fast. He always won, but he said, "You are fast and you have potential. You are determined."

That afternoon while he was leaving, I told him goodbye. He turned and waved.

"Remember what I told you," he called back to me.

"I will, I will!"

I did not see him again until a few years later when I recognized him on the movie screen. I could not believe it. I knew him from before he was a star!

Steven Seagal and me.

He was now a very popular practitioner of aikido. I met him again in 2006 in Nashville where he played blues music with his band. We spoke a little there. He seemed to remember me and invited me to stay for the show that evening.

His name was Steven Seagal. I always remembered what he told me in those earlier years. When I saw him again, I told him I was still determined. I never did give up.

He bowed his head to me, and we said goodbye for the last time.

Ann-Margret

In Florida, summer of 1979, I sang in a club in the Miami area. I learned the Miami Beach Theatre of Performing Arts had scheduled Ann-Margret to perform. She was one of my favorites since I was a child, and I dreamed of seeing her one day in person. I had remembered her ever since I saw her in *Bye Bye Birdie*. I must have seen it dozens of times in the cinema in Italy.

Now she is going to sing nearby, I told myself. I could not lose this opportunity. I decided to give her a plaque that evening like the one I gave to Elvis. I ordered it especially for her.

We performed just a few miles from the theatre, so my drummer and I decided to go meet her and bring the gift. We could not miss this chance.

While on break, I asked the manager of the club if I could leave for a few minutes. My show started at 9:30 p.m.

"Okay, but try not to be late," he said.

My drummer and I took off at lighting speed. In fact, I didn't even get the chance to change. I was still in my Elvis jumpsuit. I would be performing my tribute to him that night. My friend had said, "Why don't you leave it on and we'll just go? You don't have much time to change."

"I hope Ann will not think differently of me coming dressed as Elvis," I said.

"Well, she loved Elvis."

"I know, but I'm not Elvis."

We jumped into my car.

We arrived at the theatre around 8:45 p.m. Fans had already filled the seats and were listening to the band warming up the audience.

Everyone turned and stared at us, dressed in our entertainment clothes. We looked at each other and smiled.

My drummer said, "C'mon, let's try to get backstage."

The manager stopped us. "Are you part of the show?"

"No, sir, I'm not," I said. "I'm singing down the road, and I'm here to see Ann-Margret. I have been dreaming of this since I was little in Italy. I'm not leaving until I give her a gift."

My friend looked at his watch. "We have to hurry; you have to be back on stage soon." I waited for the response from the manager.

"Let me see the gift in that box."

I opened it and showed him the plaque.

"It's beautiful. Wait here and I'll see what I can do."

A few minutes went by. I felt my heart pounding in my chest. My friend paced nervously.

"You see, we're out of time. We'll never see her now."

"I am going to see her," I said.

All of a sudden, the manager came up. "Ann-Margret is willing to see you."

As I hurried toward the backstage, I said to the security guard, "Don't worry. Just a few minutes, and I will be on my way."

I am going to see Ann-Margret, I thought. *My dream will come true!*

My heart was beating at fifty miles a minute. I felt so nervous. What will I say? What will I tell her? She may just change her mind when she sees me dressed as Elvis. I don't know how she'll take that since she and Elvis were great friends, and now he's gone.

Up a few steps, through some halls, up more steps, more halls, and there she was! Oh, my goodness! She saw me coming. She stood with her husband, Roger Smith, also a famous actor, a celebrity from the TV series Route 66.

She looked me up and down and then smiled. I went up to her.

"It's a great honor to meet you. I loved you in *Bye Bye Birdie* and *Viva Las Vegas*. I can't believe I am next to you."

I gave her the plaque. I had been afraid she might not want to see me since I came dressed in my jumpsuit, looking like Elvis, but instead she took her time, thanked me and asked where I was performing.

Ann-Margret and me at Miami Beach Theatre of Performing Arts. Minutes before she went on, she paused for this picture with me.

117

"About two miles from here," I said. I felt for a minute that she wanted to come and see the show. It would have been wonderful, but she just wanted to know where it would be. My drummer took a photo of us. Then she told me she had to get ready. I thanked her for her time. She gave me a hug and a kiss on my cheek.

I left the club, bursting with energy. I had been near Ann-Margret, one of my favorite stars! And she gave me a kiss on my cheek!

We took off in the "bat mobile," running just a little late for my show. As soon as we arrived, I went on stage. This would not be my last meeting with Ann-Margret.

Ann-Margret in Atlantic City

In the 1980s, while I was living in New Jersey after moving from Florida, Ann-Margret performed at one of the casinos in Atlantic City. As soon as I learned of it, I immediately began working on plans to meet with her. I made sure I had the photo of us so she would remember me.

The night I arrived at the casino there was a big line backstage. I knew I would never get a chance to see her, so I decided I would ask to speak with Roger Smith. The security guard asked if he knew me.

"Yes," I answered. "They know me from the Miami Theater of the Performing Arts."

While I waited, I met Fred Travalena, a popular comedian performing as her opening act. I stopped a passerby to take my picture with him.

Me with Fred Travalena.

A few minutes later Mr. Smith came out.

"Hello. Follow me, I'll take you to see Ann."

When we came to her dressing room backstage, Mr. Smith asked me to wait a few minutes in the hall until she finished posing for photos.

"I'll tell her you're here."

Ann-Margret finally came out to me, said hello and gave me a hug.

"Are you here to see the show?"

I looked down with a sad expression.

"I was unable to get tickets."

"I'll see what I can do to get you tickets," she said.

"I'm very grateful."

"I have to leave, but wait here. I'll send someone to take you to your seat."

"Thank you," I said. "I hope that we get to see each other again."

"I'm sure we will."

A few minutes later, the usher took me to my seat. When he came up to me, he said, "There are only two seats available. They're in her friends-of-the-family section."

"Yeah?" I said. "Wow, sure!"

The usher seated me near her parents and some of her friends from Sweden. I remember it as the most enjoyable evening of my life, knowing Ann remembered me and seeing her show. What a great entertainer!

This was the last time I saw Ann-Margret. In later years, I received the telephone number of her studio and talked with Roger. Then he put her on for about a minute, and I had the opportunity to speak with her once more. I will always remember her.

Johnny Cash

I HAD THE CHANCE TO MEET JOHNNY CASH SEVERAL TIMES AND found him to be a down-to-earth person.

I will always remember him and his wife, June Carter Cash. I appeared with Johnny in a New Jersey theatre in the early '80s. I could not believe I was going to open for Johnny Cash. I recall singing a few country songs and Elvis music, plus my 45-single songs. The audience seemed to like me and at the end gave me a great, warm applause. Johnny prepared to go on after me.

As I left the stage and passed near the curtains, Johnny whispered, "You did well."

"Thanks, Johnny!"

I stayed by the curtains and watched Johnny on stage. At times, he looked toward me and smiled. I gave a wave, "Okay."

Johnny and I became friends that evening after the show. We spoke some more and had photos taken.

I told him of my trips to Nashville to record. "That's great," he said. "When are you coming again?"

"I hope soon, Johnny."

"You know," he said, "you remind me of someone that I knew well."

"Oh, really, Johnny? Who could that be?"

"Someone I worked with. We got started together."

"Oh, you mean Elvis?"

"Yeah."

I was amazed. I couldn't say anything for a few seconds. "Thanks, Johnny, for the compliment. Coming from you, it is a great honor. I will remember that!"

Johnny was so nice to pose for this picture with me.

He smiled. "You did great up there and sounded good." He gave me many compliments. I was amazed and thought to myself, Here I am standing next to this great country legend, and he is telling me all this!

"Well, I have to go," he said. "But I'm sure we will see each other again."

"You bet we will, Johnny." His wife stood next to us, listening in. She gave me a big hug, and we all said goodbye.

Australia

I LEFT FOR AUSTRALIA IN NOVEMBER 1983 TO VISIT MY MOTHER'S family. My mother took the long trip with me. We stopped at Los Angeles and Honolulu. After a two-hour layover in Hawaii, finally, the next plane would take us to Australia.

During the layover, we had dinner and went for a walk outside the airport. When purchasing some magazines, to my surprise, I saw Magnum PI. Excited, I went up to Tom Selleck and said hello.

Tom told me he was going to Los Angeles. He asked where I was going. I told him Melbourne, Australia. He wished me well on my trip.

At least three hundred people boarded the jumbo jet. After a ten-hour trip, we went through customs.

We hoped to see our relatives waiting for us. We looked all over and could not find them. Then I heard someone say my name.

"Carlo?"

I turned around and saw a young man smiling at me. He looked Italian. "Who are you?" I asked.

"I'm your cousin, Tony!"

We hugged and hugged.

We got our luggage and started the drive home where my uncle and the rest of my cousins waited. I noticed my cousin drove on the left side of the road, like in England. I began to panic.

"This is normal," my cousin told me.

For a minute, I had thought, *I just survived the plane, and now I am going to be in an accident.*

We made it home safely. When we arrived at Tony's house, a big table covered with food awaited us. I saw everyone had gathered. I loved meeting so many relatives for the first time. I had heard about them many times but had never seen them in person.

Around 7 p.m., with Mom still talking to her brother, I went to bed and fell straight to sleep. The next thing I knew, my cousin awakened me. He told me I had slept an entire day. It must have been the jet lag. It took me about four days to get used to the time difference. Also, in November, it was summer in Australia and hot while it was cold back in the States, but I got used to that fast.

The next day my cousin took me into the city. I enjoyed learning the way the people lived, seeing what they wore and hearing the Australian accents. Their voices were very friendly.

Instead of staying three weeks, we decided to stay five months. I did not want to return to the United States just yet. I really liked Australia.

I made friends and contacts to see if I could sing in some of the clubs. I could not sing for money since I did not have a work permit. I could sing free, but I needed the money. My cousin asked around to see if I could start singing somewhere. But as a visitor without a working visa, I could not find work. I would need a sponsor. My cousin could not sponsor me because we had to have a sponsor from a club or a place of work, which he could not get.

One day I went to Melbourne by myself at the time of a big Italian-themed fiesta. I decided to introduce myself at some of the radio stations in the area. The DJ at one of the stations invited me to do an interview, and then she played my record. I appreciated the exposure. That night I was heard all over Melbourne and beyond.

During my visit I became good friends with Jimmy Punturere, a singer/songwriter in the area. I went over to his house, and he had me listen to several of his songs. One was "Is It Strange." I liked it and recorded it there in Melbourne at Sound Source studios. Sound Source was owned by Rudy, the boyfriend of a singer who did backup vocals on Jimmy's record. I met her when I recorded there. While we were talking, she told me that she used to sing with Olivia Newton John. We got along well and decided that she would do some backup singing on my record. I sang with Jimmy's band, and the song aired several times on the radio. The local country radio stations in Australia were still playing my CD a decade later.

The following day I returned to Melbourne to visit some of the newspapers. I spoke with a reporter and the editor Mr. Feyne Weaver of the *Sun Magazine* and showed him my credentials. They seemed to like me and asked where I currently sang.

"Nowhere," I told them, because I didn't have a work permit. They told me they had heard me on the radio. I couldn't believe it. My article would be in the magazine the next week. I expressed my gratitude. Mr. Weaver was a great person and he gave me the chance in show business I needed in Australia. Shortly after that, I had an article written in the *Australian Post Magazine*. Mr. Weaver passed away August 4, 2008.

When I got back to my cousin's house, I let everyone know about the magazine article and when it was going to come out.

Now that I was getting my name out, I went back around to the clubs but still failed to get any work. I did sing at some weddings, happy for the great exposure.

A week later I met a man named Ernie who worked for the police department. We started talking about my career, how much I loved Australia and about my not having a work permit. He said he could book me at his club for no money. Perhaps a potential sponsor would see me. I happily sang at the Noble Park Football Club with a great band and a warm audience. They all liked me.

Me singing at the Noble Park Football Club in Melbourne, Australia.

I had one month left. The time went by very fast. I did not want to leave Australia. I tried to see as much as I could from the shores to the desert and from the clubs to the museums.

The sad day came when we said our goodbyes. Our relatives took us to the airport in Melbourne. My mom cried, and so did everyone else.

As I boarded the plane, I noticed my seat on the right side of the packed plane allowed me to see my family outside. When I saw my uncle and cousins waving goodbye, I started crying too. I must have cried for hours. Mom told me to be strong and thankful for the time we spent with them. I was thankful. I just wanted to stay.

After a nonstop flight, we landed in Los Angeles. We had one more flight to New York and then a car ride home to New Jersey.

I tried very hard to return, working three jobs and saving all my money, but in the end I stayed in America to take care of my parents. I tried to convince my father to move there, but it just did not work out. I treasure my memories of my time in Australia.

The Home of Elvis' Father

Back in the '80s, I had the opportunity to visit the home of Vernon Presley while touring the house with the new owners, friends of Gene Mason. The house was white with black shutters and located behind Graceland. Inside the gates is a garden where Elvis had planted tomatoes, and a pool is in back. The house is still in its original state today.

I went into the house and loved it. I imagined Elvis coming to visit his daddy. A road provided a shortcut to his father's house. He only had to walk behind Graceland. The house still has the original furniture, including an organ Elvis used to play. Vernon was no longer there. I wish I could have made this visit to Elvis' dad's home before Elvis died.

Me visiting in 2018
where Vernon Pressley used to live.

THE HOME OF ELVIS' FATHER

Me with Larry Strickland on the left and Gary Buckles on the right, members of the Stamps Quartet.

Perhaps everything happened for a reason—visiting Vernon's house, the friends, the family. Perhaps his spirit guided me. I know Elvis was a very spiritual and religious person. As I left the house, I waved goodbye to the owners and thanked them for inviting me.

As I was leaving the owner spoke to me. "Carlo, the house is for sale. Would you like to consider purchasing it?"

"Really? Wow! I wish I could, sir."

"Well, this would be a real dream come true for you."

"Yes, it would. I just wish I could afford it."

"Well, let me know. It's there for you whenever you like."

"Thank you," I said.

As I left I thought, How wonderful it would be if I really could live in that home! Gene continued the conversation about the house as we drove away.

"Carlo, this home is historical. You know that?"

"Yes, I know that"

"Try to buy it," Gene said.

The Home of Elvis' Father

The next day I went to the bank in Memphis and applied for a loan. I really wanted to purchase that home. I knew I would keep it forever. I did not think I would have a problem with making the payments. If only I could buy it, I thought. But the loan did not go through because I had never bought anything. I had good credit, but I did not have enough of it. I was so disappointed.

I still imagine living in that house where Elvis came to visit. Every time I visited Graceland, I drove by Vernon's home.

Me with Bill Baize, back-up singer for Elvis with the Stamps Quartet, 1978.

Ernest Tubb

While I lived in New Jersey in early 1984, I heard Ernest Tubb would be performing on a Saturday night at The Roadhouse, a club in Farmingdale.

I arrived at the club a little early to see if I could meet Mr. Tubb. The show sold out in advance. When I arrived that cold night, I noticed Mr. Tubb's bus parked near the club. I went inside and saw the warm-up still going on. I stepped back outside and went to the bus.

It must have been twenty degrees. As I walked, I felt like I was turning into a popsicle. With my personal photo and record in my hands, I knocked on the vehicle door. A friendly man who appeared to be in his 60s opened the door.

"Yes, can I help you, sir?"

I could hardly speak due to the cold. "Hello, my name is Carlo Martini. Is there any chance I could say hi to Mr. Tubb?"

"The show will be starting soon," said the smiling man. Perhaps he was Mr. Tubb's driver.

"Okay, is there any way I could say hello and give him my music I recorded in Nashville?"

As I was saying this, I heard a voice from inside the bus saying, "Bring this young man in. He must be freezing out there."

The Journey of Carlo Martini

I cannot believe I am getting on Mr. Tubb's bus. Ernest Tubb had been sitting at a small table. He stood when I entered. I must say it made me happy not only to meet him, but also because it was nice and warm in there.

"Son, you looked like you were freezing out there," said Mr. Tubb. "Come, sit down and get warm."

"Thank you. I wanted to meet you and give you my record before the show."

"Would you like some coffee to warm you up?"

"Oh, yes, I would like that." I instantly admired this kind man! We talked for a while.

"When did you record this?" he asked.

"Not long ago in Nashville."

"I like you. How would you feel if I called you on the stage tonight?"

"Oh, that would be wonderful! It would be a great honor to share the stage with you. But I didn't rehearse with the band."

"Don't worry about that, son. My musicians can back you up. You just tell them what you want to sing, and they will play it. You go on back to the show, and I'll be there shortly."

"Okay, thank you, Mr. Tubb, for inviting me on the bus and the show . . . and the coffee!"

I went back to the club. After a few minutes, he came on stage and sang several of his hits.

Then all of a sudden he said, "Ladies and gentlemen, I talked to a young boy on my bus just before the show. I would like to introduce him to you this evening."

My heart felt like it was skipping beats.

"Where are you, Carlo? There he is! Carlo Martini! Bring that young man up!"

I stepped on stage. Mr. Tubb gave me the microphone, and the band readied to play. I sang two of my favorite songs—"For the Good Times" and "Help Me Make It Through the Night."

When I finished, Mr. Tubb came up and said, "Let's give a big hand to this boy." The audience applauded, and he asked me to sing one more.

I chose an Elvis song. As I finished my third song that evening, Mr. Tubb came up, congratulated me and said, "Give a big hand to this fine boy. Thank you, Carlo."

"Thank you, Mr. Tubb."

He smiled and said goodbye.

While leaving the platform, I thought, What an honor to share the stage with Ernest Tubb, a fine man and a great legend of country music! He even took his time and introduced me. As I left the show, I saw his bus driver standing nearby.

"You did great!" he called to me.

"Thank you," I replied.

"Mr. Tubb told me to tell you if you're returning to Nashville to call or write him."

"Oh, really?"

"He would like you to sing at the Ernest Tubb Record Shop."

"I know the manager there."

"Great," he said. "I'll let him know this."

"Tell him thank you so much," I said.

I did not have a chance to travel back to Nashville until the late '80s when I appeared on the *Nashville Network*. I stopped and saw the shop and my director friend the evening of my performance, but I did not get a chance to sing there. I told the director to send my regards to Mr. Tubb.

The Ernest Tubb Theatre

IN 1994, I RECEIVED A CALL FROM THE MANAGER OF THE ERNEST Tubb Theatre.

"Can you come and sing at the Ernest Tubb Theatre? It's the *Midnite Jamboree*. You'll be heard live on radio stations all over the United States."

"Yes, sure."

"Okay, I'll see you soon."

"Thanks, I really appreciate it."

I had met the manager in the late '70s on my first trip to Nashville. He had given me help and advice when I could not find my way as a newcomer in the city.

I left Asheville that Friday on a Greyhound bus heading toward Nashville. On the bus I thought, *WOW! I am going to sing on the Ernest Tubb Theatre live radio show broadcast after the* Grand Ole Opry.

When we arrived at the station, I took a cab to one of my favorite hotels—The Hall of Fame, located near the record studios. The theatre was on the other side of town near Opryland Hotel. Next evening brought showtime!

I arrived at the theatre for the first time. Beautiful. When I entered, I saw a record shop, and the Ernest Tubb bus! Oh, that brought back memories. The knocks on the door, the freezing weather and Mr. Tubb kindly inviting me in.

The Ernest Tubb Theatre

As I continued to walk around the theatre, I heard my name called.

"Carlo!" It was the theatre manager.

"Hi, my friend." I said. "Long time no see."

"Come on, Carlo. Follow me and I'll introduce you to the band." I followed him, and he brought me to a group of musicians.

"Everybody this is Carlo. He'll be singing here this evening."

Then the director introduced me to Mr. Tubb's son, Justin. I told Justin how much I admired his dad and what a great honor it had been to be able to sing on the same stage in New Jersey.

"Thank you," he said. "Are you ready to sing?"

"Yes!"

"We're trying to get everything started for the live radio after *The Grand Ole Opry*."

While I waited, I approached Marty Stuart backstage. Oh, man! We shook hands and spoke for a little bit.

"Are you singing this evening?" he asked me.

"Yes, Marty, I am."

"Well, the time is coming. We're going to be on soon."

Some acts went on, and then came my turn to be called. Justin introduced me to the audience.

"Carlo sang with my dad," he told the audience. He really gave me a great introduction. When he had finished, he handed me the microphone, and I started singing.

When I finished, he came up and said, "Let's give a big hand to Carlo." I remembered a similar experience with his dad. Justin was saying the same thing his dad had said. I felt so honored. I thanked him and the audience and went backstage.

Marty Stuart was next. He shook my hand.

"You did well!"
"Thanks, Marty."

As I left that evening, Sam Lovullo, the producer of *Hee Haw*; and Box Car Willie, a country music singer, stood near the bus. They congratulated me on my performance. They later wrote me several times, telling me how much they liked my act.

I went directly to the station to grab the last bus leaving for Asheville. I will never forget the honor of singing at the Ernest Tubb *Midnite Jamboree.*

Wrap Around Nashville

In 1985, I got a call from Nashville Network, TNN. It was an invitation to be on the program called *Nashville Now* with Ralph Emery in a feature story, "Wrap Around Nashville." I felt eager to go back. Nashville's Bullet Recording Studios had scheduled me that week to sing my originals.

Well, I thought, why not call the TV show and have them come to the studio to film the feature story on me?

It worked out for the best, not only with *Nashville Now* but also with the feature story.

Eddy Arnold and me backstage
at the Grand Ole Opry in the 1980s.

. . .

As always, I selected a hotel near the Hall of Fame, which was also near the studio. That evening, at the Hall of Fame Hotel, I went downstairs to hear music. A great little band played in the lounge, and after I listened to them for a while, I asked the bandleader, "Is it okay if I sing a song with you?"

"Sure. Come on up."

The band let me sing two country westerns and one Elvis song. I wanted to sing because it would get me ready for the recording session. I needed all the practice I could get in front of an audience to put me in the right psychological frame of mind.

That night, sitting in the audience there in the lounge was Johnny Lee. I hadn't noticed him at first. He came up to me and said, "You did great." Then he asked me to sit down at his table.

We started talking about my upcoming appearance the next day on *Wrap Around Nashville*. He asked me where I was from, and I realized who he was. Then a man who was sitting three seats away stood up and approached me.

"Hello! I'm Wayne Carman," he said with a smile. He told me he loved the way I did the Elvis song.

My friend Wayne Carman.

I remember he impressed me as being a very polite person, although I had not heard of him. We spoke about my career and singing.

"I have to sing and record tomorrow at the studio," I told him. "I will be taped for the show."

"Terrific! What time?"

"I guess around the afternoon."

We spoke a bit more, and I told him I was a great fan of Elvis.

He smiled. "Me too!"

"Oh great!" I said. "He was and always will be the greatest legend ever."

"Yes I know." He began telling me about Memphis.

"Oh, I have been to Elvis' home many times," I said. I told him I was there in the late '70s with a friend of Elvis and his cousin Harold Loyd and others of Elvis' family.

"Wonderful."

"What about you?" I asked.

"I live there."

"Oh, really?"

"I'm a teacher of karate in Memphis."

"Oh, man, I love martial arts. Can you teach me?"

"Yes. When you come to Memphis, look me up, okay?"

"Well, did you ever meet Elvis?"

"Yes, I did. He came to the Kang Rhee Studio in Memphis where I was receiving some expert training."

"Oh really?" The more he explained his relationship with Elvis to me, the more we became friends. "Would you like to come to the studio tomorrow while I'm recording?"

"Yes, I would like that."

"Okay, I'll meet you there."

. . .

When I got to the studio the next day in the afternoon, I didn't see him there. I thought, *Where is the nice man I spoke too?* I had to start on my recording.

As I stood behind the mic, I looked up and saw Wayne Carman. I waved across the room. When I finished recording, I went right into the interview for *Wrap around Nashville.* When Wayne and I left the studio, the studio videocamera captured us exiting the doors together.

That evening had proven to be another memorable one for me, not only for the TV show, but also for my friendship with Wayne Carman. We became great friends throughout the years that followed, and I am still in contact with him today.

While I was in Nashville, I saw the Oak Ridge Boys. I had originally met them in Vegas. Later I had my picture taken in Jersey with Joe Bonsall.

Me and my friend Joe Bonsall,
one of the Oak Ridge Boys.

Back to Nashville

One day, Debra said, "Carlo, I've called your friend David McCormick, the director at the Ernest Tubb Theatre, and he told me that he's scheduled you to be on the *Midnite Jamboree*."

"Great!"

Debra booked a hotel and in October of 2010 we left for Nashville. She rented a car and came to pick me up. When we were in the car, I asked her how she started her singing career.

Debra and Randy Travis.

"I used to sing with Randy Travis?" she asked. "I met him in a restaurant, and he bought me breakfast before

I knew who he was. My brother John knew Randy when we had our band, The Downings."

She was telling me how she started singing when she was 12 with her brother. She sang with Randy Travis at Country City USA in Charlotte.

When we reached Tennessee, we put our stuff away in our rooms. We had lunch at Cracker Barrel. That's my favorite place to eat.

As we ate, we discussed what we would be doing over the following day and night. She had a lot of stuff planned for us to do before I sang. We would be going to all the record companies the day we arrived, so we left very early in the morning. We went to some recording companies on Music Row.

Debra did not want me to get too tired out, but I was so excited. She said I needed to rest before the next night so I'd be ready to go on stage. The next day we went to some more places, and that evening we were ready for the *Midnite Jamboree.*

"You're going to be going on before Jim Ed Brown."

"Wow, Jim Ed Brown. He is one of my favorite country singers."

"Jan Howard's going to be there as well," she said.

It was getting late, and we had to meet Arlene Mandrell for dinner at a place called the Nashville Palace. When we were there, Debra took a picture of us together.

Debra asked her, "What has your sister Barbara been doing?"

"Barbara just sold her house there in Tennessee," she said. We stayed and listened for a while, and then it was time to go. I told Ms. Mandrell to come over and hear me sing.

"I will Carlo if I get done here in time. I hope to see you there. Carlo, thank you and best of luck to you."

Arlene Mandrell and me at the Nashville Palace

"Thank you, Ms. Mandrell." Then she gave me a kiss on the cheek. She signed a picture for me so I signed one for her and gave her one of my CDs.

"Wow, thank you, Carlo. I will listen to this and I will check out your websites!"

I was so excited about being back in Nashville.

Debra and me at Cooter's in Nashville

David asked me to sing one of the songs I recorded. The house band from the Grand Ole Opry would accompany me. I would sing something that I was comfortable with, a song called "For the Good Times" by Ray Price. One of my favorites. I was on the stage with Jan Howard, a classic country singer from the '60s, and '70s, and Jim Ed Brown and Jean Sheppard. Backstage, I would be in the Green Room.

Jim Ed Brown and me in the Green Room.

On stage with Jan Howard.

Debra and I got to the Ernest Tubb Theatre, and the manager of the theatre showed us the Green Room. We were with the celebrities. Jim Ed Brown was very nice. We spoke there for a while. "I found you very unique, Carlo, with a different style."

"Well, thank you, sir, that is very kind."

"How did you two meet, Debra?" Jim asked.

Me at the Ernest Tubb Theatre
when in Nashville for the
Midnight Jamboree.
Photo by Debbie Poirier.

"We met in the movie business. I was producing a movie, and Carlo played a schoolteacher."

"Well, what made you become his manager?"

"As Carlo and I were talking, he told me he needed a manager, and I said yes."

Jan Howard and Jean Sheppard told me the same thing as Jim and wished me luck. Debra videotaped the whole thing for me.

Afterward, we met near the Ernest Tubb bus to sign autographs. People came up to me and asked for pictures, CDs and my autograph.

Signing autographs at the *Midnite Jamboree* with Debra.

The next morning, I needed to leave very early and went to the lobby to drop off the key. A few people were checking out of the hotel who had been at the show. They came up to me and said they had seen me and liked my singing. They followed me to the car, had their pictures taken with me and waited for my autograph. That gave me a great feeling. I did well, and they wanted to see me on the show again sometime.

While we were in Nashville, Debra called the magazine *Nashville Scene*. We spoke with the editor, Jim Ridley. I told him we were in town and asked him if we could stop by his office for an interview. Mr. Ridley told Debra he had to check his schedule.

The interview took place, and they put it in the December 22nd issue of *Nashville Scene*.

Cher

IN FEBRUARY OF 1997, I HEARD THAT CHER WOULD APPEAR at the Festival of Music Week presented every year in Sanremo, Italy. The Festival of Music highlights international celebrities. I did not have a car or anyone to take me, but I was determined to see her. I took the 6:15 p.m. train from where I was staying in Ventimiglia.

When I arrived in Sanremo, I saw a mob of people. Chaos, traffic everywhere. I got off the train as calmly as I could to keep myself from being overwhelmed. I was still determined to see Cher.

When I arrived at the Ariston Theater, she was rehearsing in the empty auditorium. I saw security guards and city police at every door. Wow, this is going to be very difficult, I thought to myself. What am I gong to do?

Luckily, I came prepared with photos, CDs, articles about me and a letter to give to Cher. I took a deep breath and thought, It is now or never. Here I go.

I found myself in front of the police who continued to talk in Italian even when I spoke in English. Often, if I spoke in English, I seemed to get a better response.

"*Scusi! Non puoi entrare,*" they said. "Excuse me! You cannot enter."

Of course, I knew what they were saying, but I pretended not to understand them. Finally, after a few minutes of my talking in English, they went to get someone who spoke English.

Luckily, the person they brought back was the manager of the show.

"May I help you?" she asked me.

"Yes, I am here from the United States to see Cher."

"Does she know you?"

"We met in the United States." (I had once auditioned on *The Mike Douglas Show* in Philadelphia when Cher performed, but I had not actually been able to talk with her that afternoon.)

"Follow me."

Oh my! I am going to see Cher. Wow! As I waited by the stage, a man came up and told me she had left.

"She has left?" I said. "I've been here forty-five minutes. You could have told me sooner."

"I am sorry," the stranger said.

I decided to try some other techniques so that I could meet her. In fact, I resolved to meet her that night. I called the hotels where the stars stayed. I told each operator I had an appointment with Cher and was going to wait for her. Finally, after calling several hotels, I learned where she stayed from some paparazzi standing near my phone booth.

When I arrived at the hotel, I found a crowd of people there. I went to the front desk.

"I have an appointment with Cher," I told the receptionist. "Has she arrived yet?"

"She is not staying at this hotel," the desk clerk said.

It was the same message I had received from the other hotels, but this time I knew it wasn't true. The person at the desk tried to get me off course. I waited in the hotel lobby. I waited and waited.

While I sat, I worked on my camera, hoping to say hello to Cher and get a photo with her. I heard a group of elderly women speaking English and introduced myself to them.

"Where are you from?" one asked.

"North Carolina," I said.

"We're from California," another said. "From Pasadena. Are you here to see Cher?"

"I have been trying all day to meet her."

"I am a friend of Cher," the third woman said.

"Do you know when she's going to show up?" I asked.

"She should be here soon."

"I looked at my camera to have it ready and realized it was broken."

The third woman volunteered, "I'll take a photo of you with Cher and send it to you."

Cher and me in Italy at the Sanremo Festival.

That made me happy. Shortly after she said that, Cher walked in and talked to her friend in the group.

I went up to her while they conversed. My heart went crazy. I could not open my mouth to say hello . . . but I had to.

"Hi, Cher," I said. "I'm your biggest fan. Can you pose for a picture with me?"

"Sure," she said. We spoke a little, while the woman with the camera took a picture. As Cher left, I gave her a kiss on her cheek. She smiled and said good-bye.

I could not believe it. I immediately went to her friend and said, "Thank you so much for your time and trouble!" I turned to the woman with the camera and said, "Thank you for the photo."

"No problem," she said with a smile. "I will send the photo as soon as I can."

"Thank you," I said. As I left the hotel, I thought, *I hope she does not lose my address. I hope the photo does not get lost in the mail.*

A month went by. Finally, one day the photo arrived in the mail. I was so happy to receive it. Without that wonderful lady from Pasadena, I would never have had my photo with Cher.

Paris

In 2000, I took the train to Paris. It's one of my favorite memories. It was my first time visiting that city.

I had a chance to sing on national TV on a show called *La Chance aux Chanson* and sang a French song! I had never worked on that song before, so I had to study fast to learn it. I took the express train to Paris from Ventimiglia Station—a seven-hour trip. The crowded train stopped along the way until Antibess, and then it took off like lighting. I became a bit tired and knew I had to relax or sleep because in another hour I would arrive in the Paris station. I did not succeed. I was so excited I could not sleep.

When I exited the train, I saw people in every direction. Taxis waited at the front of the station. I had my address ready. Using my meager French, I said, *"Prenez-moi s'il vous plaît à cet hôtel."*

"Oui, monsieur!" said the driver.

At the hotel, I could not wait to get all my things ready for the next day's TV show, but no food services were in the hotel and I was hungry. I called a taxi to take me to a nearby restaurant.

"Il y a un en environ un mile à partir d'ici," said the cab driver.

"Please tell me in English," I requested.

"There is one about one mile from here."

"Très bon," I said. I felt more tired than hungry at that point. After a light supper, I went back to the hotel and rested.

The next day I had to be at the studio at lunchtime. I needed breakfast. *Where in the world is a place nearby?* I thought. *Oh no, do not tell me I have to take the taxi again . . .*

Fortunately, when I went outside I saw a little coffee shop around the corner. Thank God, donuts were available. I must have eaten a dozen with two large coffees. I looked at my watch and still had a little time.

I browsed some shops and meditated in a park nearby until 11:00 a.m. I was hungry once more. It must have been nerves.

I went back to the coffee shop and had a sandwich. What a sandwich! In France, there are long breads. Mine was the works: tomatoes, cheese and salad with a little glass of French wine. It went down like a missile.

The crew at the TV station, where I arrived by taxi, welcomed me warmly. They took me to my dressing room upstairs.

Looking out the window, I saw a little bit of Paris. *I cannot believe I am here,* I thought.

My cousin's words came to my mind: "Someday, I'll see you on French TV." Rogero had once lived near Paris but had passed away when I was still very young.

"I'm here, Rogero," I said aloud.

The crew soon called me and we headed to the studio. I saw all kinds of cameras. In just minutes, I sang my song on the air. The studio audience seemed to like it very much, especially when I sang in French.

The day was over. I said bye to everyone, then headed back to the hotel, given a ride by the cousin of the celebrity host of the show.

"Au revoir!" I said when he dropped me off.

I went back to my room and relaxed for a while. I felt excited. Within the next month, I will have been on French TV.

That night I decided to see Paris after supper. Seeing it all in the short time left would be a challenge. Notre Dame Cathedral, the Canal Saint Martin and the Eiffel Tower looked especially beautiful at night.

I had to leave the next day on the long journey back to Italy. I had little money left and had to be careful I did not spend it all so far away from home. Not knowing anyone in Paris and being penniless could have been hard. I left by train the next morning and never returned to that beautiful city.

Author at Eifel Tower a Day before his TV
Appearance on his Birthday 2000.

The Day I Met Debra

I MET DEBRA ON A MOVIE SET. SHE TOLD ME THAT FIRST TIME ABOUT singing with Randy Travis. "I met him in a restaurant in Nashville in the early eighties," she said, "and he bought me breakfast before I knew who he was."

A poster of *A Crying Shame.*

Debra is an actress as well. She was in *A Crying Shame* and won Best Lead Actress in that is when it was born. With help of Debra, I added some more to it. The name of the movie is *TCB Thunder Missions.* We gave our company a name: TCB Thunder Motion Pictures. We were both excited about the movie.

Debra and I at Channel 21 on a TV show
in Charlotte, North Carolina.

"Morning, Carlo. How are you today? Ready to be on the show?"

"Yeah, I'm as ready as I can ever be."

She was great company and fun to talk with.

Debra knew I liked films and acting too, so one day I told her about the plan I had to write a script and that I had already done some of the writing.

"That's great," she said. "Would you like to make a movie out of it?"

"That sounds like a good idea,

I have a degree in film production.

So we both started looking over the movie and that is when it was born. With help of Debra, I added some more to it. The name of the movie is *TCB Thunder Missions.* We gave our company a name: TCB Thunder Motion Pictures. We were both excited about the movie.

The ActionFest was an annual film festival in Asheville, North Carolina. Both Chuck (action movie superstar) and Aaaron Norris (martial artist) were present in 2010 and 2011.

Aaron Norris and me at Actionfest.

Chuck Norris and me at *ActionFest* in Asheville.

Western Movie Appearances

I recently acted in a country and western movie called *Vengeance Without Mercy*. It came out in 2018 and 2019 respectively. It is directed by Chris Forbes from Georgia. I played the ghost of a tough guy who had been named "Carlos."

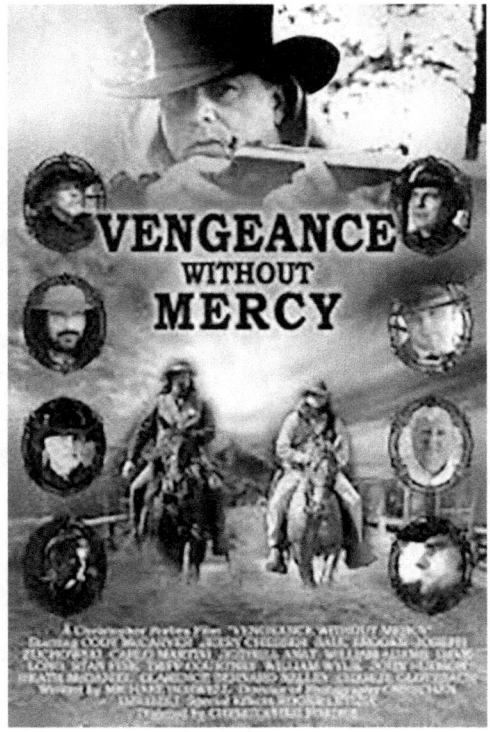

Carlos ←

MOVIE APPEARANCES

On the set of *Billy the Kid* as as Mr. Carlo Polermi.

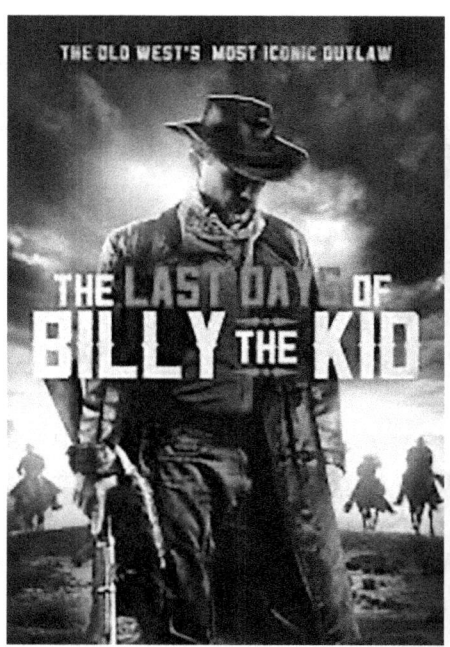

Some scenes were filmed in Love Valley, North Carolina.

I played Mr. Carlo Polermi in *Cheat the Hangman*. Some scenes were filmed in South Carolina.

Tom Jones and Engelbert Humperdinck

I REMEMBER WHEN I WAS YOUNG IN ITALY AND USED TO VISIT MY favorite cinema, I once went to see the James Bond film *Thunderball* and liked the singer of the theme song. I greatly admired his power and style. What a voice! I had to investigate to find out more about him.

I learned his name was Tom Jones. I went immediately to search for his records. At first, I could not find any except for the *Thunderball* theme, but after a while, I found more and more of his music. I started listening to "Thunderball" repeatedly and daydreaming. I was so impressed. I told myself, *One day I'm going to meet him and sing his songs.*

Many years elapsed. When I lived in the US in the late '60s, I still listened to him and hoped one day I could meet him.

The dream came true for me on several occasions.

One of those times was in the late '80s when Tom was playing at the Garden State Arts Center in New Jersey. I went to see him but had a difficult time approaching him because of the crowds and the tight security. However, later that night, I went backstage. He walked by me and said, "Hi."

In 1987, I heard he was appearing in a casino in New Jersey. I made special arrangements this time to meet him. I sent a fax to the casino and to his personal secretary, explaining my situation and that I had wanted to meet him since I was little. Later that day, I received a call and a fax stating Tom would have time to see me during his show.

The next day was Saturday. I left home at 5:15 p.m. The trip to Atlantic City would take me two hours by car from my home in Farmingdale, New Jersey. However, it was well worth it.

While I drove, I could not stop thinking that I was finally going to meet Tom Jones and that he was expecting me. I kept remembering when I was little how I would dream about meeting him. And now it would finally come true.

As I pulled up in my Cadillac, I looked like I was arriving for a wedding. All dressed up in a great suit. I was ushered in. I approached the backstage entrance and saw the police security. I introduced myself and gave them the letter. I felt as nervous as a bird sitting on a little wire in a windstorm. I was shaking. I just did not know what I would say to Tom when I saw him.

The security guard said, "What can I do for you, sir?"

"Well, I'm here to see Tom," I said. "I have this letter stating that he is expecting me."

"Okay, does he know you?"

"Well, not really," I replied. "This will be my first time meeting him."

"Okay," he said and took my letter.

I thought I waited for an hour, but it was not that long. The guard finally returned and said Tom would see me.

Oh, my goodness, here I go, I thought. I walked through a few halls and doorways, and there he was.

Tom shook my hand. "How are you?" he asked.

"Ah . . . Tom, it is a great honor to meet you." I told him of my childhood in Italy. I told him how much I had admired him from a very young age. He listened with interest to what I said. We spoke for a bit. I found him to be a very gracious person.

Tom Jones and me,
photo taken at Harrah's in Cherokee, North Carolina.

I said, "Thank you so much, Tom, for your time."

"No worries," he said.

I turned away.

"I'll be downstairs in the private lounge," he called after me. "Would you like to join me for dinner?"

I could not believe my ears! "Yes, I would love to. Where would you like to meet and when?"

He appeared about to tell me when his manager said, "I'm sorry, but we can't."

I was in shock by his remark. Tom invited me and his manager said no. Tom looked at me.

"Sorry, Carlo. Maybe there will be another time we can meet and talk."

"Oh, sure, Tom. Thanks anyway. Bye." As I left the casino, I felt very upset with the situation, but at least I was able to meet Tom. In that regard, my dream came true.

Earlier the same year, I had met Engelbert Humperdinck during his performance at an Atlantic City Casino.

Engelbert Humperdinck with me in Atlantic City.

Another encounter with Tom was in Sanremo, Italy. He performed at the Festival of Sanremo in 2000. I got the chance to say "hi" once again. He recalled our last meeting and was very polite.

The last time I would get to see him was in Cherokee, North Carolina, at Harrah's Casino in 2008. I spoke to the director of the casino to get permission to go backstage. After the director and I exchanged several faxes, Tom Jones apparently was contacted, and I received a special invitation to go backstage and meet him. Once again, our friendship was renewed. He invited me to stay and see the show. I had no tickets, but his management people made sure I would be able to go in.

Tom is a great singer and entertainer. He was a friend of Elvis Presley. That made it all the more special for me to be his friend. I added one of his songs to my act out of my deep admiration for him.

Me with Bon Jovi at an annual
music festival
in Sanremo, Italy, in 1988

On the Italian Riviera

I LIVED ABROAD IN ITALY INTERMITTENTLY FOR SEVERAL YEARS IN a small town on the seafront. My mother and father lived there, so I decided to spend most of 1987 in Italy. I tried to take care of my dad and mom when I could, but occasionally I had to leave.

Toward the end of 1987 and on into 1988, I sang in some clubs in Italy and appeared on several talk shows on TV Rai—Italian national television. I also did many radio interviews.

When not called to perform on stage, I sang at times nearby at the ristorante called "Tempio Della Musica" in Vallecrosia.

Train is a stage at the Tempo Della Musica Restaurant in Vallecrosia, Italy.

The owner, Erio Tripodi, has since passed away. The restaurant became a meeting place for many celebrities of Italy when they visited town—notables like Pavarotti and the prince of Monaco.

The restaurant had a big locomotive train in front, great food and music, and a recording studio in the back. The owner called me several times during my years in Italy to sing for the Friday and Saturday events.

I appeared once at the Theatre Smeraldo. It is well known as a performance site for many singing stars, both Italian and international. I sang there for a full house in memory of Elvis one evening. There were many "Italian Elvises."

It took about four hours to get there, always traveling in trains when I went long distances. Once I arrived, a taxi waited to take me to my destination. I worked with several Italian celebrities over the years, including Gianni Morandi and Maria Teresa Ruta.

While visiting Monte Carlo in 1987 and singing at one of the clubs, I had the pleasure of meeting a woman from Monaco, Countess Madame Rosy Astor. She came to hear me sing a few times, and we became friends.

One day she told me that they were filming in Monaco an Italian picture produced by Luigi de Laurentiis.

"Really?" I said. "It sounds great. I wish I could be in it."

She looked at me and smiled. "I'll see what I can do."

"Really? Do you know the producer?"

"I do. I will talk to him."

"Okay. Thank you Madam Astor."

One week later she called me at home in Italy. "Can you take the train and be here in Monaco tomorrow at 2:00 p.m.? We have an appointment to meet Mr. Laurentiis."

"Really . . . oh my God."

"Please make sure you're here," she said.

"Yes, Countess Madam Astor, I will. Where do I meet you in Monaco?"

A photo and poem Madame Astor gave to me.

"At Hotel de Paris." It is a very well-known hotel for many guests—from celebrities to royal personalities and others.

I could not believe I was actually meeting Mr. Laurentiis there . . . whoa! Dreams do come true.

"Thank you, Madam Astor. I will be there."

. . .

I recall I arrived at the train station at 1:35 p.m. I was so excited to meet Mr. Laurentiis. I could not believe it. He actually was going to speak with me personally! My appointment was at 2 p.m. I immediately took a taxi so I would not be late.

The taxi took me to the front doors of the Hotel de Paris, a very nice hotel.

As I entered the doors, it felt like I was walking into another world. It was elegant and had a very wealthy look. I waited for Countess Madam Astor. A few minutes later, there she was.

"Bonjour, Carlo," said Countess Madam Astor. "Are you ready to meet Mr. Laurentiis?"

"Yes . . . I am ready as I can be."

But deep inside I was trembling. My legs were about to give in . . . however, I knew this was going to be good for me, and I tried to stay calm.

We walked up the stairs to his suite and were invited in. I was welcomed with Madam Astor. There he was.

"You must be Carlo," he said.

"Yes, sir, it's me."

"I heard about you. Countess Madam Astor told me about you."

I was thinking inside of me, *My goodness, Countess Madam Astor. She told him of me.* And here I was . . . I was so grateful.

"So, Carlo. I hear you sing and act."

"Yes, sir." I told him a bit of my life and career. He seemed to like me and started to ask more questions.

"Carlo, how would you like to be in my film, *Montecarlo Gran Casinò?*"

"Yes, I would like that very much."

"Although I wish I could put you in a speaking role, the script is already done. But I can add you as an extra in front of the cameras. There will be casino shots that you will be seen in and shots in the restaurant in Menton, Le Pirate . . . would you like to be in it?"

"Yes sir," I said without thinking twice. "I would like that very much. Thank you for giving me the chance."

"Okay, Carlo. We start filming Monday for two weeks here in Monaco. Can you be here at 8 a.m. on the set?"

"Sure," I said. "I'll be there."

"Okay, I will tell them in casting you are in on the payroll."

"Okay, thank you."

I was thanking him so much. I just could not believe Mr. Laurentiis gave me an opportunity to be in the film.

"I will not let you down. I promise, okay?"

"I'll see you Monday," he said.

Madam Astor was happy. "Voilà," she said with a smile. "You're in."

"Thanks to you . . . see you Monday."

The following Monday, everyone from the cast and crew met to film inside the Casino of Monte Carlo. I was working with actors including Christian de Sica, a celebrity of Italy and son of the famous Vittorio de Sica; Massimo Boldi, a comedian; and film actor Ezio Gregio, also a comedian actor.

I traveled a short train ride every morning from Ventimiglia, Italy, to the filming in Monte Carlo.

I recall the first morning of shooting. Everyone gathered early to prepare for a long day ahead. To stay calm, I meditated and prayed.

My moment came.

"*AZIONE!*" said the director. "Action!"

The scene took place in a casino. Some people were at the roulette table at the bar.

We did another scene with the leading stars in Restaurant Le Pirate, the restaurant in Menton, France. Despite being only an extra, I enjoyed becoming friends with some of the celebrities. We filmed for about three weeks and then I left for home.

Montecarlo Gran Casinò was out in December. I went to see it in the local theatre in Sanremo. As I sat there, several people recognized me. After the showing, they came up to me, shook hands and asked for my autograph. "I'm not the star of the show," I said. But I thought, *What a nice feeling!* That feeling has always stayed with me.

I was an extra in the Italian Movie *Gran Casino* in 1987 with Laurenti Productions.

On this trip, I had the pleasure of talking with Bon Jovi at one of his concerts. He called me backstage when he learned I was in the audience and from South River, New Jersey. He had attended a school near mine.

In 1988, I had another great experience working on a film with Steve Martin and Michael Caine called *Dirty Rotten Scoundrels*. The set was on the Côte d'Axur, France, on the Riviera. It took a week to film the casino scene I was in, from 8 p.m. in the evening to early morning. I walked around by the roulette tables where Michael Caine and Steve Martin were gambling. It was a great moment.

I was an extra in one scene of *Dirty Rotten Scoundrels* with Steve Martin and Michael Caine

Sonny Shroyer

I was in Asheville, North Carolina, in 1989, at the Radisson Hotel. I had been invited to sing at a film festival with several celebrities. I would perform on the same stage as Sonny Shroyer. One of my favorites, Sonny was Enos on *The Dukes of Hazard.* It was a special evening for me. I arrived at the Radisson around 8:25 p.m. A large crowd had gathered. The dinner and the show had started.

I noticed Enos standing to my left. Oh, man! I was so happy to see him. He stood among a group of old pioneers of western films. I saw Judy Taylor, John Boy's sister in *The Waltons,* standing with them.

What a great evening! The house lights dimmed, and the show started. The celebrities went up on the stage in turn, to give a speech, sing or accept various honors.

My turn came. I sang a few songs. Everyone seemed in great spirits that evening. They enjoyed my singing.

The show would be over at 11:30 p.m. As I left to sit back down at my table, I noticed people moving around to talk to various stars. I decided to approach Sonny and introduce myself.

"Hi, Mr. Shroyer. My name is Carlo Martini."

"Hi, how are you?"

He took time with each of his fans as he signed autographs.

I went on around the room to meet the other celebrities including those from *The Waltons* and the old western films. I noticed Sonny seemed ready to leave, so I said goodbye to the other VIPs and went to speak with him again at the front check-in-area.

My mother, already a big fan of his show, accompanied me. She loved him so much. Sonny seemed to like her also.

"I'll make you a big pizza," she told him.

Sonny laughed and carried on. He gave me the feeling that he really enjoyed our company. More people were coming up to him, asking for a photograph. He turned to me and said, "Can you wait a second? I'll be right back."

Sonny really liked my company and agreed to take a picture with me.

I was impressed by Sonny, and I was very happy to have started a friendship with him. After taking the photograph with his fan, he came back to us.

"Well it's getting late, and I need to leave early in the morning."

"I'd like to give you my number," I said. "And if you like, give me a call sometime."

"Sure, I will," he said. He hugged my mom, and we shook hands.

I asked him if he would take a photo with us. He looked at me and smiled. "Sure."

As we left that evening, I thought, *I'll probably never get a call from him.*

Well, to my surprise, a couple weeks later we got a call from Sonny Shroyer. *Enos is calling me!* We must have talked for forty-five minutes. He spoke with my mom too. I asked if it would be okay to call him in the future. He said he was fine with that.

Due to my being in Italy off and on for several years, I did not see Sonny for a while, but I still kept in contact with him.

I was booked at another show with Sonny. When he saw me, he called, "Hey, how ya doin', buddy? We're on the same show!"

"Yes, that's great!" I said.

After the performance, our friendship grew. We went out to eat with my friends Elaine, who owned the Stitch in Time Shop, and Cliff, the inventor of the miracle cloth. We ate at Carrabbas in Asheville.

Elaine made a few of my Elvis jumpsuits. She also had a costume shop in the mall as well in Asheville.

When we arrived at the restaurant, we met Sonny outside. "Good to see you, buddy," he said to me with a smile.

I was so happy to be in the company of Sonny Shroyer! After we sat down and placed our order, people started to recognize him and came to the table for his autograph. We laughed a lot. He was so funny. We had chicken, fish, salad and apple pie with ice cream.

Sonny had mussels. "I just love the mussels here at Carrabba's. This is a nice restaurant."

Oh boy, I enjoyed the food, but I enjoyed even more having dinner with Sonny! We left the restaurant around 10:45 p.m. and took him back to the hotel where my friends and I took more photos and said goodbye. Everyone went their separate ways.

Sonny and me with Elaine McPherson in 1997,
in front of Carrabba's in Asheville.

The next morning I received a call from Sonny. He asked if I would come visit and bring my mom. My mom made a giant pizza for him. We called his room when we got to the hotel to let him know we had arrived.

"Can you come down?" I asked him. "We'd like to say goodbye."

"Why don't you come on up?"

So my mom and I and the pizza headed up to Sonny's room. We knocked at the door and Sonny answered.

"Hi, buddy! Hi, Mama Nina! What you got there?"

"I made a big pizza for you!" she said.

"Oh, man, you didn't have to go to all that trouble."

"Well, I promised you I would make you a pizza, and I wanted to give it to you."

Sonny gave her a big hug. We spoke a bit, and then he said, "How am I going to get on the plane with this big pizza? I guess we have to start eating it now, and I can save some for later."

"Okay," we said.

After sharing slices of pizza, we all went downstairs and said our goodbyes at the front door. I feared I would not see him again, but I was thrilled to see him again in Cooters in Nashville. I gave him one of my *Carlo Country* CDs. His *Dukes of Hazzard* car, General Lee, was on display.

Sonny and me in Nashville when he congratulated me on my *Carlo Country* CD.

Me with General Lee, car used in *Dukes of Hazzard*.

Cherokee, North Carolina

A FEW DAYS AFTER I RETURNED TO ASHEVILLE, I CALLED DEBRA. I told her about a contest in Cherokee that would take place on July 22, 2011, at Harrah's Cherokee Casino. It was the annual Elvis Tribute Artist show. I asked her if she wanted to go.

"Okay, Carlo, that sounds great."

Debra came up on the weekend that I was going to the contest. When we were at the casino, I was feeling a little nervous. Debra told me, "Hey, Carlo, just say you've done this before, and you're going to do it again. Now go get them. Remember." She is always encouraging me and telling me to think positively.

Everyone that afternoon and evening was getting ready for the show. Seeing all the Elvis Tribute artists gave me a wild sensation. Keeping the legend alive. Everyone that night performed with passion. I went backstage and spoke with some of the tribute artists. It was great to participate in the show.

Debra is always positive no matter what. She believes in me and knows the potential that I have. She sees it in me sometimes. I don't always, but she sees beyond what I see. Sometimes when I think things are not going right, Debra is there to tell me not to give up, to keep on going and not to have negative thoughts.

Debra keeps me busy doing my singing and acting. She has brought a lot of happiness into my life.

My tribute to Elvis at Harrah's

While I was at the Elvis event in Harrah's Cherokee Casino, I was happy to see Sam Thompson, Elvis' former bodyguard. He had been invited as a guest to speak about Elvis. I reminded him of speaking to him in Florida when I gave Elvis a gift. He recalled the incident.

Sam Thompson and me at Harrah's.

My tribute to Elvis
at the Orange Peel
in Asheville in 2015.

Back to Memphis

Debra called me one day and said The Hard Rock Café in Memphis wanted me to perform on August 14, 2011. While I was there, she landed me another job at the American Legion. I realized that the more I was around Debra, the more I had fun working with her. She was a great manager.

She entered me in a contest for Elvis tribute artists called "King of the World." We stayed in the Marriott in Memphis. The show was downstairs in the ballroom. It turned out to be a great event in honor of Elvis, and it was nice to meet all the other artists.

Debra had been working so hard for me and had been getting so many things done that I decided to surprise her and take her to Graceland. She had never seen it before. She was happy. She told me I didn't have to do it, but I wanted to.

I took her to see Vernon's home behind Graceland. When we drove up, we saw two ladies taking flowers out of the back of a pickup truck. The truck was parked in front of the house on the street.

I pulled the car over, and Debra and I talked about the house for a while. After a few minutes, the ladies noticed us. I decided to go meet them. Debra was afraid to bother them so she stayed in the car.

I introduced myself and began to talk with one of them. She was the owner. I said I had been there before in the early '80s and had wanted to buy the house, but I couldn't get a loan from the bank. I described what the house was like back then. I explained that there used to be tomatoes in the garden that Elvis had planted for his father. She said they weren't there anymore. She had never known about them.

I was about to say goodbye when she stopped me.

"Carlo, would you like to come in and look at the house?"

"Oh, wow, sure!" I ran back to the car. "Debra! She said we can go in!"

Debra looked surprised. "Really?"

The owner gave us a private tour of the house. It was a great feeling. We saw all the bedrooms upstairs. Priscilla and Elvis' little stepbrothers slept upstairs sometimes. I felt welcome there as we walked through the hallways and rooms.

Then the owner showed us the living room where Elvis visited his daddy. As she was talking, I began to have a strange feeling. I began to feel like I was going back in time. I could hear what she was saying, but it was like I was in another world. I was in the living room back in the '60s on a hot summer day. I saw Vernon sitting on the couch in a cutoff t-shirt. Elvis was standing in front of him.

The owner led us to the kitchen. We passed by a fishbowl with money inside it, sitting on a little wooden table. It was a donation jar. Debra and I put in a dollar.

"It's really ironic," said the owner.

"What?" asked Debra.

The owner looked at me. "It's amazing how much character you have in yourself that reminds me of Elvis."

I didn't know what to say. "Thank you very much," I said. "That's a nice compliment."

We went into the kitchen. The owner told us that Elvis used to make peanut butter and banana sandwiches there. They were his favorite. She pointed to a chair by the dinner table. "That was where he used to sit. You can sit down in it if you want, Carlo." I walked over to the chair and sat down.

"Did you know Elvis?" asked Debra.

"I met him a couple times," said the owner. "I was a friend of Vernon's. I used to spend time hanging around with the family."

"What was he like?"

The owner didn't say anything for a moment. "His mannerism was wonderful. He was a nice person and pleasant to be around. He never showed me any disrespect."

We stayed a little while longer and then said goodbye. When I thanked the owner, she gave me a hug and said, "Whenever you're in Memphis, come back again."

She walked outside with us to the white brick fence. It was a nice day in Tennessee. There were only a few clouds in the sky.

The next day, I bought something for the owner. A bottle of champagne and a box of chocolate biscuits. We drove to the house, and I knocked on the door. The owner answered.

"I wanted to thank you again for letting me come in and see Vernon's home."

"You're most certainly welcome." She hugged me and thanked me for the gift. "You know, I'm having a get-together that will be going on over the next couple days. People will be coming and going as they choose. You're welcome to come by if you like. A few celebrities will be here. Some of Elvis' cousins will be stopping by, too."

"Thank you," I said. "I would love to, but we have to return home."

"Well, have a safe trip back," the owner said. She smiled. "It was good seeing you again, Carlo."

Debra and I got in the car. I looked at the house one more time, and we headed home.

Me at Graceland in November 2018.

Acknowledgments

I thank Debra for her patience and guidance in development of this book as well has her fine photography of many of the pictures included. I thank Micki and the rest of the team at Grateful Steps for years of sharing my vision as we worked on this book. I also thank everyone who is mentioned in this book.

www.ingramcontent.com/pod-product-compliance
Lightning Source LLC
LaVergne TN
LVHW020929090426
835512LV00020B/3274